The Harlem Renaissance

An Explosion of African-American Culture

Other titles in the America's Living History series:

Alamo
Victory or Death on the Texas Frontier

ISBN-13: 978-0-7660-2937-8
ISBN-10:   0-7660-2937-9

The Fascinating History of American Indians
The Age Before Columbus

ISBN-13: 978-0-7660-2938-5
ISBN-10:   0-7660-2938-7

Space Race
The Mission, the Men, the Moon

ISBN-13: 978-0-7660-2910-1
ISBN-10:   0-7660-2910-7

The Harlem Renaissance

An Explosion of African-American Culture

Richard Worth

Enslow Publishers, Inc.
40 Industrial Road
Box 398
Berkeley Heights, NJ 07922
USA
http://www.enslow.com

Library of Congress Cataloging-in-Publication Data:

Worth, Richard.
 Harlem Renaissance : an explosion of African-American culture / Richard Worth.
  p. cm.—(America's living history)
 Summary: "Explores the Harlem Renaissance, a reawakening of African-American culture, including literature, the arts, theater, and music, motivated by a goal to achieve equal rights"—Provided by publisher.
 Includes bibliographical references and index.
 ISBN-13: 978-0-7660-2907-1
 ISBN-10: 0-7660-2907-7
1. African Americans—Intellectual life—20th century—Juvenile literature. 2. Harlem Renaissance—Juvenile literature. 3. African American arts—20th century—Juvenile literature. 4. African Americans—History—1877–1964—Juvenile literature. 5. Harlem (New York, N.Y.)—Intellectual life—20th century—Juvenile literature. 6. African Americans—New York (State)—New York—Intellectual life—Juvenile literature. 7. African American arts—New York (State)—New York—History—20th century—Juvenile literature. 8. New York (N.Y.)—Intellectual life—20th century—Juvenile literature. I. Title.
E185.6.W884 2008
700.89'9607307471—dc22

                              2007025593

To Our Readers: We have done our best to make sure all Internet addresses in this book were active and appropriate when we went to press. However, the author and the publisher have no control over and assume no liability for the material available on those Internet sites or on other Web sites they may link to. Any comments or suggestions can be sent by e-mail to comments@enslow.com or to the address on the back cover.

♻ Enslow Publishers, Inc., is committed to printing our books on recycled paper. The paper in every book contains 10% to 30% post-consumer waste (PCW). The cover board on the outside of each book contains 100% PCW. Our goal is to do our part to help young people and the environment too!

Contents

These soldiers of the 369th Infantry Regiment, also known as the "Harlem Hellfighters," won a French medal called the Croix de Guerre for gallantry in action during their World War I

Chapter 1

Marching in Harlem

On January 1, 1918, as a heavy snowstorm battered the coast, a regiment of African-American soldiers landed in France. The regiment came from Harlem, New York.

They had struggled through a long voyage across the stormy Atlantic Ocean in a leaky ship for more than six weeks. When they finally arrived in France, the men of the 15th Infantry Regiment, New York Army National Guard, expected to be rushed up to the front lines. World War I had been raging across eastern French soil since 1914. The Allies—Britain, Russia, and France—faced the veteran soldiers of the Central Powers, which included the Austro-Hungarian, German, Ottoman, and Bulgarian empires. Both sides had dug in along two thousand miles of trenches that stretched from the North Sea to the Swiss border. Over four years, they had battered and bloodied each other. Each side lost hundreds of thousands of men in a vain attempt to score a knock-out victory and win the war.

Finally, in 1917, the United States entered the struggle on the side of the Allies. This would tip the scale—it was hoped—against Germany and the rest of the Central Powers. During the months leading up to war, military units had already begun training across America. The 15th New York, however, was different from most other regiments. It was the brainchild of a group of African-American leaders. They built the regiment from black volunteers in Harlem—a section of New York City where many African Americans lived. Charles W. Fillmore, a prominent lawyer with military experience, sponsored the regiment.

At this time, many whites looked down on blacks and regarded them as second-class citizens. Regulations, called Jim Crow laws, discriminated against African Americans. The laws were named after a nineteenth-century black character performed onstage by a white man. He smiled and shuffled along and treated whites as his superiors. Under the Jim Crow laws, society was segregated, meaning there were separate facilities and institutions for blacks and whites. Blacks were not permitted to enter many hotels, restaurants, or theaters. These were reserved for whites only. African Americans had to enter bus stations and other public facilities through doors for blacks only. They also were prevented from voting, although black men had been given that right in a constitutional amendment.

The 15th tried to recruit volunteers with a parade led by a well-known black comedian named Bert Williams. But white New Yorkers who went to the parade made fun of them.[1] The governor of New York, John Alden Dix, even refused to provide any funds to buy uniforms and rifles for the regiment. Finally, he allowed the regiment to recruit volunteers. But this happened only when the Harlem organizers of the regiment agreed to let a white political leader, William Hayward, become commander of the unit.

COLORED

A boy drinks from a water fountain in Halifax, North Carolina. Only African Americans could use this water fountain.

Hayward recruited many white officers and a few black officers. Perhaps the best-known was Lieutenant James Reese Europe. Born in Mobile, Alabama, in 1881, Europe had demonstrated an unusual gift for music from early childhood. In New York, Europe played a type of popular music called ragtime. This was an early form of jazz. Europe appeared in clubs and theaters along Broadway. He formed orchestras and produced musical comedies. These included *The Shoo-Fly Regiment*, which was about the participation of African-American soldiers in the Spanish-American War.

Europe also took a prominent role in urging African-American leaders to use music as a way to boost the position of blacks in society. He was appointed the leader of the 15th Regiment's band.

Preparing for War

The band marched through the streets of New York in an effort to recruit men to the 15th Infantry Regiment. But African Americans were divided over whether they should fight for a nation that practiced discrimination. One man who saw the band said, "They'll not take me out to make a target of me and bring me back to Jim Crow me."[2]

But many African-American leaders believed that blacks must join the army and fight. Then they could prove that they were the equals of whites and achieve equality. This was the position of Adam Clayton Powell Sr., the eloquent minister of the Abyssinian Baptist Church in Harlem. "This is the proper time for us to make a special request for our constitutional rights as American citizens," Powell said. "The ten million colored people in this country were never so badly needed as now."[3]

Many African Americans agreed. The 15th Regiment swelled to over two thousand men. Recruits signed up from New York and surrounding areas. Among them was John Graham, a shipping clerk. There was also Hannibal Davis, only fifteen and too young to join, but who pretended to be older. Spottswood Poles played center field for the New York Lincoln Giants—a local Harlem baseball team. And Noble Sissle was a song-writer who played the bandolin. This was a combination of the mandolin, banjo, and snare drum. He became a member of the regimental band and later a famous jazz composer.

During 1917, the regiment trained in New York. Then they were shipped to Camp Wadsworth in Spartanburg, South Carolina. The whites in that town were not eager to have a black regiment in their midst. Across the South, the Jim Crow laws ensured that blacks remained segregated from whites. As Spartanburg's mayor, John Floyd, stated, the blacks of the 15th "will probably expect to be treated like white men. I can say

right here that they will not be treated as anything except Negroes. We shall treat them exactly as we treat our resident Negroes."[4]

In Spartanburg, the soldiers of the 15th felt the sting of racism. One of them was kicked off the sidewalk by a group of white residents and pushed into the gutter. Noble Sissle entered a white hotel to buy a newspaper where he was rudely treated by the owner. "Say, nigger, don't you know enough to take your hat off?" the owner said. Sissle was not going to put up with this kind of treatment. He realized that white soldiers in the hotel were wearing hats. That is "a government hat," he told the burly hotel owner. But the man would not listen and physically kicked Sissle out of the hotel.[5]

There were other incidents in Spartanburg, before the men of the 15th were finally shipped north and boarded a troop carrier for France.

Over There

Once the African-American soldiers arrived in France, Colonel Hayward hoped to bring his men up to the front lines. World War I had been raging for four bloody years, and the Allied troops were nearing exhaustion. But American leaders had other duties in mind for an African-American regiment. The men were given axes and shovels and ordered to build railroad tracks. These

Lieutenant James Reese Europe conducts the 369th Regimental Band outside the American Red Cross Hospital No. 9 in Paris in 1918.

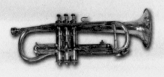

would be used to transport the waves of U.S. troops that would be arriving in 1918.

Hayward and other officers were extremely disappointed. It was considered an honor to serve on the front lines. They contacted political friends in the United States and tried to pull strings to move the 15th Infantry Regiment into combat. Nothing worked, until Hayward hit on another strategy. James Europe and his band went on tour to towns and cities across France. They became a big hit and brought instant fame to the 15th Infantry Regiment. As a result, the men were finally assigned to the front lines. The men of the regiment now felt that they were being given the same honor as white soldiers.

The 15th became part of the American Expeditionary Force (AEF) and was renamed the 369th Infantry Regiment. The men of the 369th longed to prove themselves. But they received a rude shock when they reached the western front in France. Rains soaked the landscape, turning the roads into a muddy mess. When they reached the front lines, they discovered that four years of warfare had made the trenches into rat-infested holes.

The American soldiers soon realized that they were unprepared for the ugly face of modern war. Massive artillery bombardments exploded through the sky, keeping men underground to preserve their lives. Some of the shells contained poison gas, like mustard gas or phosgene. They caused a soldier's skin to blister, interrupted his breathing, and finally resulted in his death. The men of the 369th had a lot to learn, and the French were willing to teach them. Unlike Americans, the French were color-blind, meaning that they did not regard the black soldiers as inferiors. They welcomed them into the front lines. French soldiers taught them how to use gas masks to protect themselves from the German attacks.

The Harlem "Hell Fighters" of the 369th Infantry Regiment fought valiantly during World War I. They are depicted in this painting by H. Charles McBarron.

The 369th was serving in the lines that ran along the Argonne Forest, near the French city of Reims. Black regiments were kept separate from the white regiments in the trenches. Early in the morning of May 14, the Germans launched a raid against the position held by the 369th. Barbed wire ran along the line in front of the trenches. But, under cover of darkness, German soldiers approached the wire and began cutting it.

Henry Johnson and his buddy Needham Roberts were defending the trench as the Germans entered it. Soon the entire position was lit up as hand grenades exploded. Although Roberts was wounded, he gave his grenades to Johnson. Johnson threw them at the Germans. But German soldiers entered the trench and tried to take Roberts prisoner. Johnson drove them off, killing two of the Germans in hand-to-hand combat.

As Roberts and Johnson were taken to the hospital, word of their bravery reached Colonel Hayward. Newspaper reports were sent back to the United States, where both men became instant heroes. The French army awarded each man the Croix de Guerre, (Cross of Battle). This was a medal for bravery in combat. As one newspaper in Harlem claimed, with these medals, "the Negro has vindicated his character as a fighting man."[6]

But the heroism of the 369th did not end with this single incident. The German offensive continued during June, followed by an Allied counterattack. As the 369th advanced into the Argonne, the Germans mounted a blistering fire. The French accompanying the American regiment began to retreat. They called to Colonel Hayward, "Retire! Retire!" But Hayward yelled, "My men never retire. They go forward or they die!"[7] The 369th stood its ground and stopped the German assault.

Victory and a Parade Down Broadway

During the summer, the German army exhausted itself in an unsuccessful attempt to achieve success. The war finally ended with an Allied victory in November 1918. The 369th Infantry prepared to sail for New York. Before leaving, each soldier received the Croix de Guerre for bravery. Upon returning to New York, Colonel Hayward planned to stage a parade, celebrating the success of the African-American regiment. The men had proven that they were the equal of any white soldiers. Indeed, they had outperformed many white regiments that had gone to France.

On the morning of February 17, 1919, the 369th Infantry marched down Broadway in full uniform. Along the sidewalks were thousands of New Yorkers who had come out to see them. As one man who skipped work put it, "I just had to see these boys. I never will get another opportunity to see such a sight, and I can get another job."[8] Ahead of the soldiers stepped

17

James Reese Europe, leading his world-renowned band. The regimental drum major was Bill "Bojangles" Robinson—a well-known dancer and jazz performer. The band started by playing a French military song. But as the parade continued north and entered Harlem, the music changed. Suddenly, the musicians struck up a popular song, "Won't You Come Home, Bill Bailey." Crowds of Harlem residents surrounded their hometown heroes.

The victory of Harlem's own soldiers and the performance of its famous band became a symbol of black pride. This pride would form the center of a cultural revolution that was soon to follow. It would be known as the

Members of the 369th Regiment arrive in New York by ship in 1919 after fighting on the front in World War I.

Harlem Renaissance. This explosion of culture was in a variety of forms—literature, music, theater, and painting. The Harlem Renaissance gave voice to a desire among African Americans for social and political equality. It also changed the way the rest of America viewed the African-American experience.

Chapter 2

Beginnings

Shortly after World War I ended, an editorial called "Returning Soldiers" appeared in the African-American magazine *The Crisis*. The article was written by the magazine's editor, William Edward Burghardt Du Bois. W. E. B. Du Bois was a strong advocate of equal rights for African Americans. "We are returning from war!" Du Bois wrote in an editorial:

> We sing: This country of ours, despite all its better
> souls have done and dreamed, is yet a shameful land.
> It *lynches*. . . .
> It *disenfranchises* [deprives people
> of the vote] its own citizens. . . .
> It encourages *ignorance*. It has never really
> tried to educate the Negro. . . .
> It *insults* us. . . .
> We *return*.
> We *return from fighting*.
> We *return fighting*.
> Make way for Democracy! We saved it in France,

and by the Great Jehovah, we will save it in the United States of America, or know the reason why.[1]

Perhaps more than any other man, W. E. B. Du Bois initiated the Harlem Renaissance. The Harlem Renaissance was a cultural movement based on pride in the African-American experience. No longer were African Americans willing to be second-class citizens. They demanded equality with whites.

A Civil Rights Pioneer

Du Bois helped lead the civil rights effort. Born in 1868, he grew up in Great Barrington, Massachusetts, a picturesque village tucked into the New England hills. Few African Americans lived there. Young Du Bois experienced little prejudice. Then, one day an unpleasant incident occurred in his elementary school. "In a wee wooden schoolhouse," he wrote:

. . . something put it into the boys' and girls' heads to buy gorgeous visiting cards—ten cents a package— and exchange. The exchange was merry, till one girl, a tall newcomer, refused my card. . . . Then it dawned upon me with a certain suddenness that I

21

was different from others. . . . shut out from their world by a vast veil.[2]

Nevertheless, Du Bois did not allow this experience to stand in his way. He eventually left Great Barrington. An exceptionally bright young man, he entered Fisk University in 1885. This is a college in Nashville, Tennessee, that was founded for African Americans. But in Nashville, Du Bois experienced the full burden of racial segregation in the South. This persuaded him to devote all of his intellectual talents to ending it.

Du Bois left Fisk after graduation and went to Harvard University. In 1895, he became the first African-American student to receive his Ph.D. "I was in Harvard," he later said, "but not of it."[3] Du Bois felt separate from the rest of the students, who were mostly white. Over the next few years, he taught at Wilberforce, an African-American college in Ohio, and at the University of Pennsylvania. Then he went to Atlanta University in Georgia.

W. E. B. Du Bois's book *The Souls of Black Folk* made an impression on African Americans, because he described the way many of them felt about being black in the United States.

In 1903, Du Bois published a powerful book titled *The Souls of Black Folk*. In this book he wrote of African Americans, "One ever feels his two-ness—an American, a Negro; two souls, two thoughts, two un-reconciled stirrings: two warring ideals in one dark body, whose dogged strength alone keeps it from being torn asunder."[4] Du Bois meant that black people wanted the same equality that other Americans enjoyed. But, as blacks, they were made to feel inferior. They were objects of "personal disrespect and mockery, . . . ridicule and systematic humiliation. . . ."[5]

In 1909, Du Bois became one of the founding members of the National Association for the Advancement of Colored People (NAACP). The NAACP dedicated itself to ending racial discrimination. Du Bois also became the founder and editor of its magazine, *The Crisis*.

The magazine grew from a circulation of one thousand to a subscription rate of over fifty-five thousand by 1919. Much of this was due to the sharp-tongued Du Bois, who tirelessly called on African Americans to protest injustice. "By the God of Heaven," he wrote, "we are cowards and jackasses if now that the war is over, we do not marshal every ounce of our brain and brawn to fight the forces of hell in our own land."[6]

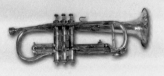

Growth of Harlem

Du Bois ran *The Crisis* from his office in Harlem, a New York City neighborhood that was rapidly becoming a center of African-American culture. Harlem had been a sleepy little community founded by the Dutch in the seventeenth century. Gradually, the size of Harlem had swelled with immigrants who came from Europe during the 1800s. By 1880, an elevated subway rattled along Eighth Avenue into the west side of Harlem. In 1904, a subway was dug under Lenox Avenue, which connected Harlem to the center of Manhattan.

More and more people could now commute from Harlem to their jobs in lower New York City. By this time, many prosperous Jews lived in Harlem. Many had moved into newly built apartments while others had built fashionable homes. Some of these homes were designed by one of New York's leading architects, Stanford White.

All this began to change around 1903, when a recession hit the real estate market. Too many homes had been built for the wave of new residents who were supposed to be coming to Harlem. But their numbers were much smaller than the builders expected. To fill the buildings, a smart, twenty-four-year-old African-American real estate broker named Philip Payton had an idea. He encouraged African Americans who lived in other parts of Manhattan to move north to Harlem.

"My first opportunity came as a result of a dispute between two landlords," Payton said. "To 'get even' one of them turned his house over to me to fill with colored tenants. I was successful in renting and managing this house, after a time I was able to induce other landlords to . . . give me their houses to manage."[7] The local white home owners were furious. They did not want African Americans moving into their neighborhoods. They held protest meetings and tried to keep out the African

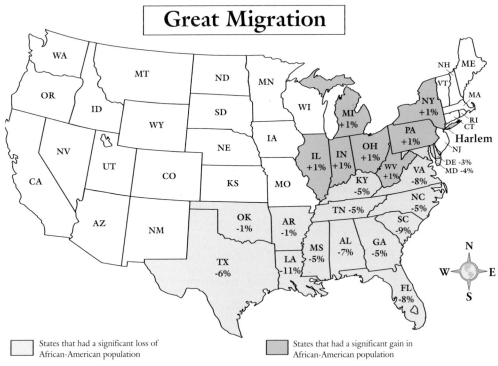

Great Migration

States that had a significant loss of African-American population

States that had a significant gain in African-American population

Americans. But the effort failed, and droves of white home owners started moving out of Harlem.

During the next decade, a large number of African Americans began moving to Harlem from the South. One reason for the move was an economic depression in the South. Cotton farms were devastated by a plague of boll weevil insects and severe floods that ruined the crops. Meanwhile, World War I had begun. German submarines clamped a blockade around western Europe. As a result, the steady stream of immigrants who sailed the Atlantic to America could no longer reach its shores. This increased the demand for other workers in the North. African Americans could more than triple their wages by leaving the South and running machines in northern manufacturing plants.[8] These plants made supplies for the Allies during the war.

Thousands of African Americans headed north. By 1920, Harlem had seventy-three thousand African-American residents. This was two thirds of all African Americans living in New York City.[9] The larger part of this increase was due to African-American migrants who left the rural South for the urban life of northern cities. They were joined by black immigrants coming to the United States from the Caribbean.

Unlike most other northern city neighborhoods, however, Harlem was mostly African-American. This made Harlem different. In his short story "City of

Refuge," author Rudolph Fisher wrote about the impact of Harlem on his main character Gillis. Gillis has just seen Harlem for the first time:

> Gillis set down his tan-cardboard . . . case and
> wiped his black, shining brow. Then slowly, spread-
> ingly, he grinned at what he saw: Negroes at every
> turn . . . big, lanky ones; men standing idle on the
> curb, women, bundle-laden, trudging reluctantly
> homeward, children rattle-trapping about the
> sidewalks. . . . There was assuredly no doubt of his
> where-abouts. This was Negro Harlem.[10]

James Weldon Johnson

Harlem became a symbol for African Americans. This was a place where they could be themselves and take pride in being black. James Weldon Johnson, who was a prominent member of the Harlem Renaissance, may have summed it up best. He wrote:

> So here we have Harlem—not merely a colony or
> a community or a settlement—not at all a 'quarter'
> or a slum or a fringe—but a black city located in
> the heart of white Manhattan, and containing
> more Negroes to the square mile than any other
> spot on earth. It strikes the uninformed observer

Paul Laurence Dunbar (1872–1906)

Paul Laurence Dunbar was an African-American writer considered to have influenced the Harlem Renaissance. Born in Dayton, Ohio, in 1872, Dunbar almost became an attorney. But instead he decided to dedicate himself "to interpret my own people through song and story. . . ."[11] In 1896, he published a highly acclaimed book of poetry called *Majors and Minors*. Critics praised Dunbar's so-called dialect poetry. This was written in the speaking style used by poor, uneducated African-American slaves. It portrayed them as happy-go-lucky plantation workers who were well treated by their masters. Many whites believed that this was the way blacks felt about slavery.

While Dunbar appreciated the wide acceptance of his dialect poetry, he wanted to write other things as well. But magazines and book publishers seemed uninterested. "I am tired of dialect," Dunbar said, "but the magazines aren't. Every time I send them something else they write back asking for dialect."[12] Some of Dunbar's material dealt with racial prejudice. Among these works was the story of a young black man who believed that his college degree would help him enter the white world. However, he discovered that these doors were closed to him. In his last novel, *The Sport of the Gods*, Dunbar wrote about urban life among African Americans. As his setting, Dunbar chose the street life in the African-American neighborhoods of New York City.

as a phenomenon, a miracle straight out of the skies.[13]

Born in Jacksonville, Florida, in 1871, James Weldon Johnson enjoyed a comfortable childhood. His mother was a schoolteacher at a highly rated African-American grammar school. Johnson's father had worked hard to become the head waiter at a prestigious white hotel. Johnson attended Atlanta University—a leading African-American institution—and then came home to run the grammar school where his mother had taught for so many years. It was a local-man success story, but Johnson soon became restless. The life of a school principal was not exciting enough for him.

Johnson and his brother Rosamond began writing music. With school closed in the summer, the brothers traveled to New York, the center of the music business. James Weldon Johnson composed "Lift Every Voice and Sing" in 1900. This song became known as the "Negro national anthem." It celebrated the first thirty-five years of freedom from slavery in 1865. Eventually, Johnson and his brother left the South to live permanently in New York. There they wrote successful musicals that were staged on Broadway.

Johnson also became involved in African-American politics. He met Booker T. Washington, one of America's most prominent African-American leaders. Washington

and Du Bois were on opposite sides of African-American political thought. Du Bois wanted to fight racial discrimination by whites. Washington tried to get along with them. He said that blacks could not expect to have social equality with whites until they had achieved economic equality. In 1881, Washington founded the Tuskegee Institute in Alabama for African Americans. The curriculum emphasized vocational skills, so students could support themselves in better paying jobs after graduation.

Washington quickly recognized Johnson's enormous intelligence and his commitment to improving the lives of African Americans. Washington was a friend of Theodore Roosevelt, who had become president of the United States in 1901. Through Washington's influence, Johnson received an appointment to the U.S. Foreign Service under Roosevelt. From 1906 to 1912, he represented the United States in two Latin American countries, Venezuela and Nicaragua.

During this same period, Johnson wrote poetry and had it published in prestigious American magazines. He also completed a novel, *The Autobiography of an Ex-Colored Man*, in 1912. The book vividly described the experience of a light-skinned black man who pretended to be a white. A friend had urged the character to try to pass as white: "My boy, you are by blood, by appearance, by education, and by tastes a white man. Now why do

Charles W. Chesnutt (1858–1932)

A writer publishing at the same time as Paul Lawrence Dunbar was Charles W. Chesnutt. Born in Ohio, Chesnutt later supported himself as a court reporter. Meanwhile, he wrote short stories that appeared in leading magazines. In 1899, two books of these short stories were published. These described the tragic lives of black slaves, forced to endure insensitive white masters. In one story, a slave returned home to discover that his master had sold off his wife to another plantation. Some of Chesnutt's stories also dealt with the racial prejudice encountered by African Americans after slavery was abolished. These former slaves had left the South to live in northern cities.

In his novel *The Marrow of Tradition*, published in 1901, Chesnutt described a race riot. Race riots actually occurred across the South and in many northern cities during the late nineteenth and early twentieth centuries. The main characters in Chesnutt's novel found themselves cruelly trapped by white prejudice. One man who tried to get along with whites lost his son in an attack by a white mob. Other characters refused to give in to the whites. They were also treated brutally. In *The Colonel's Dream*, written in 1905, Chesnutt portrayed a man who tried to overcome racism in his hometown. Instead, the white townspeople forced him to leave the community.

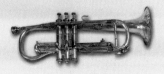

you want to throw your life away amidst poverty and ignorance, in the hopeless struggle, of the black people in the United States?"[14] White society accepted the character. Nevertheless, the man felt that he had betrayed his own heritage by pretending to be someone else.

Stressing Education

After his novel's publication, Johnson joined W. E. B. Du Bois at the NAACP. Johnson became the director of the organization in 1920. Both Du Bois and Johnson were part of an unofficial group of African Americans called the "New Negro." These were talented, well-to-do, highly educated African Americans. Du Bois called them the "Talented Tenth." He believed that at least 10 percent of each generation of African Americans should be educated. According to Du Bois, these extraordinary individuals should be trained to lead the rest of the African-American race to equality. Du Bois said:

> How then shall the leaders of a struggling people be
> trained and the hands of the risen few strength-
> ened? There can be but one answer: The best and
> most capable of their youth must be schooled in
> the colleges and universities of the land. . . . All
> men cannot go to college but some men must. . . .
> He is, as he ought to be, the group leader, the man
> who sets the ideals of the community where he

lives, directs its thoughts and heads its social movements.[15]

These leaders, according to Du Bois and Johnson, should be shining examples of how much African Americans could accomplish. They should also take pride in their African heritage. In the past, Americans had looked down on this heritage as inferior to white culture, which had been inherited from European immigrants who came to America. The New Negro movement celebrated the African heritage and emphasized its important role in shaping American culture.

Du Bois also urged African Americans to write about their unique experience. Their society had been forged by the fires of slavery. Only they knew the harsh realities of trying to succeed in a white world where they constantly faced discrimination. Instead of remaining silent, as they had in the past, Du Bois urged them to be heard. "A renaissance of American Negro literature is due," he wrote, "the material about us in the strange, heart-rending race tangle is rich beyond dream and only we can tell the tale and sing the song from the heart."[16]

The Champions of Culture

Among the people whom Du Bois invited to Harlem to tell this story was Jessie Redmon Fauset. Fauset became one of Du Bois's editors in 1919 when she was

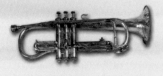

thirty-seven. Born in 1882, Jessie was one of seven children of a Presbyterian minister, Redmon Fauset, and his wife Annie. The family lived outside Philadelphia, although Jessie attended the High School for Girls in the city. She was among the best students in her class. But, as the only African American, she continually felt the sharp sting of racial prejudice. Nevertheless, Fauset applied to Cornell University in New York, where she became the only African-American woman on campus. Graduating at the top of her class in 1905, she taught high school in Washington, D.C. In 1919, she moved to Harlem and took the position of literary editor at *The Crisis* magazine.

Children play in the streets of Harlem in the 1920s.

From her position as literary editor of *The Crisis*, Fauset became one of the key leaders of the Renaissance. During the Harlem Renaissance, Fauset would publish the works of many young writers in *The Crisis*. She also wrote essays for the magazine and published her own novels.

In addition to Fauset, another leader of the

Renaissance was Alain LeRoy Locke. Locke was born in Philadelphia in 1886 and later attended Harvard University. He graduated at the top of his class in 1907. Locke then traveled to England to study at Oxford University on a Rhodes Scholarship. These scholarships are awarded to outstanding young scholars in the United States. Locke was the first African American to win this prestigious award. Like Fauset, he was highly educated and extremely talented.

After returning from England, Locke began teaching at Howard University, an African-American institution in Washington, D.C. He remained at Howard for over thirty years. Nevertheless, he found time to play a key role in the Harlem Renaissance. Locke wanted to break down the stereotypes that had plagued African Americans for many years. Among these was the shuffling, happy-go-lucky character, grinning at white people while he served them as a waiter or janitor. According to Locke, this was just a role that African Americans had learned to play. It reinforced the view among whites that black people were inferior. Instead, Locke urged African-Americans to be themselves. According to author Nathan Huggins, "the new militancy" that Locke supported among African Americans "was a self-assertion as well as an assertion of the validity of the race."[17]

Locke, Fauset, Johnson, and Du Bois asserted a new sense of black pride. They laid the foundation of the Harlem Renaissance that began in the early 1920s.

Chapter 3

Writing About the Black Experience

In 1919, poet Claude McKay wrote:

If we must die—let it not be like hogs
Hunted and penned in an inglorious sport,
While round us bark the mad and hungry dogs,
Making their mock at our accursed lot.
If we must die, O let us nobly die,
So that our precious blood may not be shed
In vain; then even the monsters we defy
Shall be constrained to honor us though dead![1]

McKay's poem "If We Must Die" was written in response to the vicious race riots that ripped across America in 1919. Whites rampaged across East St. Louis. They killed forty African Americans, including a baby. Rioters were afraid that black factory workers hired during the war were taking jobs away from whites. In Ellisville, Mississippi, three thousand spectators watched an African American accused of rape being lynched by the local sheriff. A lynching is an execution of a person by mob action without legal sanction.

Riots also broke out in Longview, Texas; Omaha, Nebraska; and Washington, D.C. Riots had occurred in the past, but the 1919 riots were different. This time African Americans fought back.

Claude McKay

Born on the Caribbean island of Jamaica in 1889, Claude McKay later became one of the leading poets of the Harlem Renaissance. One of eleven children, he began to demonstrate his unusual gifts as a child. While attending elementary school, he wrote poetry. Claude's early poems drew on his Jamaican heritage as well as the hymns he sang in church. As a teenager, he lived with an older brother who taught school in a Jamaican village. McKay continued writing poetry, and his fame spread across the island. By the age of twenty-two, he had published two books of his poems. These were *Songs of Jamaica* and *Constab Ballads*.

In 1912, McKay left Jamaica, hoping to achieve greater recognition in the United States. He attended Tuskegee Institute. After only a short time there, McKay left for Kansas State University. While a student there, he read W. E. B. Du Bois's book *The Souls of Black Folk*. McKay later said that it "shook me like an

37

earthquake."[2] After only two years in Kansas, McKay left the campus and began traveling across the United States. He worked as a waiter and dishwasher to support himself. During his travels, he also came face to face with racial discrimination.

In 1914, McKay went to Harlem. "It was like entering a paradise of my own people," he said.[3] McKay hoped to become part of the literary scene. He met a few white magazine publishers. But very little of his work ever appeared in their magazines. Finally, most likely in 1917, he met Max Eastman. Eastman was the white publisher of a socialist literary magazine called, *The Liberator*. McKay's poem "If We Must Die" was published in *The Liberator* two years later.

By 1921, Max Eastman was so impressed with McKay that he asked the young poet to become co-executive editor of the magazine. While working at *The Liberator*, McKay also published a book of poems called *Harlem Shadows* in 1922. With this book, "McKay instantly acquired the status of being the first significant black poet since Paul Laurence Dunbar," wrote literary critic Stephen Watson.[4] *Harlem Shadows* is

Although he was originally from Jamaica, Claude McKay accurately captured the rich culture of Harlem in his writings.

one of the most important works of the early Harlem Renaissance. McKay's poems express the many facets of the black experience. In one of his poems, "The Negro's Friend," McKay wrote:

What waste of time to cry: "No Segregation!"
When it exists in stark reality,
Both North and South, throughout
this total nation,
The state decreed by white authority.[5]

For McKay, however, success did not bring him the satisfaction he hoped to achieve. McKay never forgot the bitter impact of discrimination that he had experienced in his travels throughout the United States. He always felt inferior to whites. As he wrote in his poem "The White House":

Your door is shut against my tightened face,
And I am sharp as steel with discontent;
But I possess the courage and the grace
To bear my anger proudly and unbent.[6]

In 1922, soon after the publication of his book, he left *The Liberator*. McKay also left America in 1920 to live in England. In 1922, he moved to the Soviet Union. In 1917, a revolution led by communists destroyed the

Walter Francis White

A novelist of the Harlem Renaissance, Walter White was born in Atlanta, Georgia, in 1893. Although several of White's ancestors were black slaves, the rest were whites. The blond, blue-eyed White often passed for a white American. Nevertheless, he recognized that he was black.

White dedicated most of his life to improving the position of African Americans. In 1918, he went to work for the NAACP as the assistant to James Weldon Johnson. A year later, Johnson sent him south to report on a riot in Phillips County, Arkansas. In his spare time, White became a novelist. In 1924, he published *The Fire in the Flint*. In this novel, White told the story of Kenneth Harper, a doctor in a small Georgian town. Harper was a representative of the Talented Tenth. Harper believed that "If he solved his problems and every other Negro did the same . . . then the thing we call the race problem will be solved." Unfortunately, Harper became the victim of a lynching by Southern whites. *The Fire in the Flint* became a best-seller and made White a famous writer.

In addition to writing, White provided support and encouragement to other Harlem Renaissance writers like Claude McKay. After Johnson left the NAACP, White became its director. He remained at the NAACP until 1955, the year of his death.

Russian monarchy. Russia became the Soviet Union, preaching equality for all its citizens. "Never in my life did I feel prouder of being an African, a black, and make no mistake about it, I was like a black icon [hero]," McKay said.[7]

From the Soviet Union, McKay traveled to Europe. There he published the novel *Home to Harlem* in 1926. In this novel, McKay presented everyday life in Harlem. He emphasized its music, its nightlife, and the lifestyles of its working people. One of his main characters, Ray, described Harlem this way: "Harlem! . . . the rich blood-red color of it! The warm accent of its . . . voice, the [fruitiness] of its laughter, the trailing rhythm of its 'blues' and the improvised surprises of its jazz."[8]

After living in France, Spain, and Morocco, McKay returned to America in 1934.

Searching for Identity

While he served as editor of *The Liberator*, Claude McKay looked at hundreds of manuscripts. They were submitted by young writers who wanted to be published in the magazine. One of these writers was Jean Toomer. The thin, handsome, almost white-skinned Toomer was born in 1894 in Washington, D.C. After his parents died, Jean grew up in the home of his grandfather, the legendary Pinckney Benton Stewart Pinchback. After the Civil War, African Americans received the vote and some

of them won election to public office. Among them was P. B. S. Pinchback, lieutenant governor and later governor of Louisiana. After leaving the governor's mansion, Pinchback moved to Washington, D.C. He became part of a group, which included Alain Locke, that taught at Howard University. Jean Toomer went to Dunbar High School, where Jessie Fauset had taught before going to New York.

But Toomer was not happy with his role in society. He felt conflicted between being an African American and being almost white in skin color. Toomer left Washington, hoping to find himself. He attended several colleges, dropping out of each one. He also worked at a variety of jobs. For a time, he sold Model T Ford automobiles. He became a bodybuilder and taught physical education. "I have worked, it seems to me," Toomer said, "at everything: selling papers, delivery boy, soda clerk, salesman, shipyard worker, librarian-assistant, physical director, school teacher, grocery clerk, and God knows what all."[9] None of these jobs seemed to satisfy him. Eventually, he went to New York City, where he met a group of poets, writers, and editors at a party. They inspired him to begin writing.

Meanwhile, Toomer needed to support himself. He heard about a position in Sparta, Georgia, as principal of a local agricultural school. Toomer took the job and lived with other African Americans in Sparta. There, he listened to their stories, shared their lives in poverty, and attended their churches. "When I live with the blacks, I'm a Negro," he said. "When I live with whites, I'm white, or better, a foreigner. I used to puzzle my own brain with the question. But now I'm done with it."[10]

Toomer accepted his African-American identity and wrote about his experiences. After returning to New York, he lived in Harlem. There, Toomer produced a series of short stories and poems. Meanwhile, he met Alain Locke. Locke published some of Toomer's poetry in *The Crisis*. At the same time, Toomer was writing his only book, *Cane*, published in 1923. *Cane* combined poetry and fiction with Toomer's experiences in the South. One part of the book described six women from the South. The second part depicted the efforts of African Americans to improve their lives by moving to northern cities.

In *Cane*, Toomer presented "a portrait of an educated, confused black, an artist struggling to represent the parting soul of the African-American past in art."[11] As Toomer wrote in "Song of the Son":

O Negro slaves, dark purple ripened plums,
Squeezed, and bursting in the pine-wood air,
Passing, before they stripped the old tree bare
One plum was saved for me, one seed becomes

An everlasting song, a singing tree,
Caroling softly souls of slavery,
What they were, and what they are to me,
Caroling softly souls of slavery.[12]

The book was widely praised. As one critic put it, "Jean Toomer is a bright morning star of a new day of the [black] race in literature."[13]

Only a few hundred copies of the book were sold. Nevertheless, it inspired many other writers of the Harlem Renaissance. Unfortunately, *Cane* was so difficult for Toomer to write that he never produced another book.

Nella Larsen

Nella Larsen was another leading writer of the Harlem Renaissance. She was born in Chicago in 1891. Her father was a black West Indian and her mother was white. After Larsen's father disappeared, her mother married a white man. But having a partly black child was very difficult for Larsen's step-father to accept. This created great sadness for Nella. Indeed, it helped inspire her novel *Quicksand*.

As she said of her main character, "She saw herself for an obscene sore in all their lives, at all costs to be hidden."[14] Larsen's mother sent her to Fisk and Tuskegee universities. Larsen went to New York in 1912 where she became a librarian and a nurse. She published *Quicksand* in 1920, and it was hailed by W. E. B. Du Bois. He called it "the best piece of fiction that Negro America has produced since the heyday" of writers like Charles Chesnutt.[15] In her second novel, *Passing*, Larsen wrote about a young black woman who passed for white. Larsen eventually traveled to Europe. When she came back to Harlem, she had stopped writing and returned to nursing.

Countee Cullen

Among the African-American poets inspired by *Cane* was twenty-year-old Countee Cullen. Young, talented, good-looking, with perfect manners, Cullen seemed to be a symbol of the Talented Tenth. But his background had been somewhat different. He was born Countee Porter in Louisville, Kentucky, in 1903. His father abandoned the family, and his mother soon left the South. She took her son to Baltimore to live with her mother-in-law. Countee and his grandmother later moved to New York.

After his grandmother died, Countee was adopted by the Reverend Frederick Asbury Cullen. The Reverend Cullen was pastor of Salem Methodist Episcopal Church in New York. Countee adopted the Reverend Cullen's last name and began writing poetry. Countee was recognized as a so-called "poet prodigy" while still a teenager.[16] He published poems in high school and at New York University, where he received many honors. These included Phi Beta Kappa for academic excellence. While still in college, his poems also began to appear in widely read literary magazines. They included *Harper's*, *Century*, and *American Mercury*. Cullen spent much of his time in Harlem, where he met other African-American writers like Jessie Redmon Fauset.

Cullen was widely praised by the African-American community for his work. But he had not escaped the

sting of discrimination by whites. They often made him feel like a second-class citizen. Cullen wrote about these experiences in his poem, "Incident":

> *Once riding in old Baltimore,*
> *Heart-filled, head-filled with glee,*
> *I saw a Baltimorean*
> *Keep looking straight at me.*
>
> *Now I was eight and very small,*
> *And he was no whit bigger,*
> *And so I smiled, but he poked out*
> *His tongue, and called me, "Nigger."*
>
> *I saw the whole of Baltimore*
> *From May until December;*
> *Of all the things that happened there*
> *That's all that I remember.*[17]

Nevertheless, other poems like "Harlem Wine" celebrated the joy and excitement he discovered in Harlem.

Langston Hughes

Among Countee Cullen's closest friends was someone usually considered the most famous poet of the Harlem Renaissance. Born in Joplin, Missouri, in 1902, his name was James Mercer Langston Hughes.

Langston Hughes poses with a small statue in 1943, long after he had made a name for himself as a poet of the Harlem Renaissance.

His grandfather had fought with John Brown at Harpers Ferry in 1859. Brown and his men had tried to begin a slave uprising in the South. But they were caught and hanged.

Hughes's parents, Carrie and James Nathaniel, fought continually. Finally, all of their arguing ended in divorce. Hughes did not feel close to either parent, and felt unloved by both of them.

An important person in young Langston's life was his grandmother. She read *The Crisis*, and Langston soon became familiar with the writings of W. E. B. Du Bois. After his grandmother died, Langston and his mother moved to Cleveland.

He had a rare gift for poetry and began writing poems in elementary school. At Central High School in Cleveland, he met the daughter of novelist Charles Chesnutt. She helped Langston refine his work.

In 1921, his first poem appeared in *The Crisis*, "The Negro Speaks of Rivers." But Hughes's early success could not make up for the fact that he often felt sad—a result of his childhood. As he once put it, he wrote "mostly because, when I felt bad, writing kept me from feeling worse."[18]

Like other writers of the Harlem Renaissance, Hughes had also experienced discrimination. He wrote:

I, too, sing America.

I am the darker brother.

They send me to eat in the kitchen

When company comes.

But I laugh,

And eat well,

And grow strong.

To-morrow

I'll sit at the table

When company comes

Nobody 'll dare

Say to me,

"Eat in the kitchen"

Then.

Besides, they'll see how beautiful I am

And be ashamed,—

I, too, am America.[19]

In this poem, Hughes combined the pain he suffered in the past with a determination to assert his pride in being an African American. These two elements lay at the heart of the Harlem Renaissance.

Hughes did not join the writers of the Harlem Renaissance immediately. He came to New York initially to attend Columbia University. But college did not excite

Charles S. Johnson (1883-1956)

Sociologist Charles S. Johnson attended college in Richmond, Virginia, and served in the infantry during World War I afterward. He returned to the United States after the war and enrolled at the University of Chicago for graduate study. One of the worst race riots of 1919 erupted in Chicago while Johnson was attending college. Afterward, Johnson was selected to serve as associate executive secretary to a commission that wrote a report on the riot.

After the report was completed, Johnson traveled to New York. He had been selected to be the editor of a magazine called *Opportunity*. It was published monthly by the Urban League. Founded in 1910, the Urban League was devoted to ending racial discrimination and segregation in America. Although Johnson supported the goals of the Urban League, he believed that the African-American struggle would take many years. Nevertheless, Johnson realized that in one area African-Americans could achieve equality. This was in the field of the arts.

Therefore, Johnson opened up the pages of *Opportunity* to the work of gifted black poets and writers. He also began to promote black artists to his white friends. Johnson realized that their support was essential to broaden the audience for African-American literature. Some of his friends were influential civic leaders who sat on the board of the Urban League. He brought them together with the poets and writers of the Harlem Renaissance to create a great flowering of culture.

him. Instead he found himself spending more and more time in Harlem. There, he met Countee Cullen and other writers. Soon Hughes dropped out of Columbia and decided to support himself by working as a deckhand on a freighter. Meanwhile, he continued to write, sending his poems to Cullen. Among them was "The Weary Blues." This poem, written while he worked aboard ship, captured the rhythms of street life in Harlem. Hughes described the nightclubs, jazz bands, and theaters that were springing up in Harlem.

In June 1922, Hughes's ship left New York, headed for a long voyage to Africa. Sailing along the coast, he at last began to experience his African heritage. He experienced life among the people of Africa and their proud history. This great sense of pride found its way into a series of poems. Among these was "The Negro Speaks of Rivers."

I've known rivers:
I've known rivers ancient as the world and
older than the flow
  of human blood in human veins.

My soul has grown deep like the rivers.

I bathed in the Euphrates when dawns were young.

I built my hut near the Congo and it lulled
me to sleep.
I looked upon the Nile and raised the pyramids
above it.
I heard the singing of the Mississippi when
Abe Lincoln went
　　down to New Orleans, and I've seen its
　　muddy bosom turn
　　all golden in the sunset.

I've known rivers:
Ancient, dusky rivers.

My soul has grown deep like the rivers.[20]

From Africa, Hughes went to Europe. He visited Paris, France, as well as Venice and Genoa, Italy. In 1924, he returned home to Harlem to publish his poems. These became part of the literature of the Harlem Renaissance.

Chapter 4

A Flowering of Culture

O n the evening of March 21, 1924, Charles S. Johnson arranged a lavish dinner under the glittering lights of New York's Civic Club. It was one of the few posh restaurants in New York that admitted both whites and blacks. Artists and activists of the Harlem Renaissance came together with leading publishers and magazine editors. Among the guests were W. E. B. Du Bois and Countee Cullen. The master of ceremonies for the evening was Alain Locke.

Johnson had held the event in part to honor Jessie Fauset. She had just published a novel titled *There Is Confusion*. As one reviewer said, "The author of *There Is Confusion* can write. No one who reads this story can fail to recognize that fact. This book can be read with immense profit by white and black alike."[1]

The characters in Fauset's book symbolized the values of the Talented Tenth. They believed that African

A band plays at Harlem's Savoy Ballroom in the 1930s.

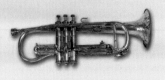
Americans could overcome discrimination by their brilliance and hard work. As one character related:

> The time comes when he [an African American] thinks, 'I might just as well fall back . . . a colored man just can't make any headway in this awful country.' Of course, it's a fallacy. And if a fellow sticks it out he finally gets past it, but not before it has worked considerable confusion in his life.

Philip, a character in the novel, had fought in World War I. He believed that African Americans had to fight their battles with a positive attitude:

> Our battle is a hard one and for a long time it will seem to be a losing one but it will never really be that as long as we keep the power of being happy . . . . Happiness, love, contentment in our own midst, make it possible for us to face those foes without. "Happy Warriors," that's the ideal for us.[2]

The dinner at the Civic Club provided a meeting place for white and black cultural leaders. Charles Van Doren, who was editor of *The Century Illustrated Monthly Magazine*, talked about the flowering of African-American writers. Countee Cullen read one of his poems, and a leading publisher agreed to publish a book of Cullen's poetry. Paul Kellogg, editor of the influential *Survey Graphic*, told Charles S. Johnson that he wanted to dedicate an upcoming issue of his magazine to *The New Negro*.[3]

Edited by Alain Locke, *The New Negro* was released in 1925. It celebrated Harlem as a center of African-American culture. "Harlem has become the greatest Negro community the world has known. . . . It is—or promises at least to be—a race capital."[4] Locke urged his readers not to think of African Americans as "something to be argued about, condemned or defended, to be 'kept down,' or 'in his place,' or 'helped up,' to be worried with or worried over. . . . Until recently, lacking self-under-standing, we have been almost as much a problem to ourselves as we still are to others."

But Locke added that the "thinking few" had "renewed self-respect and self-dependence . . . in the life-attitudes and self-expression of the Young Negro, in his poetry, his art, his education, and his new outlook."

Over forty-two thousand people, white and black, read *The New Negro* published by *Survey Graphic*. The publication helped spur enormous interest in the Harlem Renaissance.

The Harlem Renaissance in Full Flower

In 1925, Charles S. Johnson hosted another important dinner at Fifth Avenue's Civic Club. This time he awarded the first annual prizes from *Opportunity* magazine. The judges for these prizes were among the most distinguished white writers in America. They included humorist Robert Benchley as well as best-selling author Fannie Hurst. Among the winners was up-and-coming African-American author Zora Neale Hurston, who won several awards.

Born in 1901, Hurston grew up in Eatonville—a small African-American community in Florida's heartland. Her father was elected mayor of the town. As a child, Hurston listened to the stories being told by the people who shopped at the Eatonville general store. Later, she wove these stories into her fiction. After her mother died when she was nine, Hurston went to Baltimore and lived with relatives. Following her graduation from high school, she went to Howard University. One of her professors was Alain Locke. He became so impressed with her writing that he introduced her to Charles S. Johnson. At Johnson's suggestion, she moved to New York. In 1924, her short story "Drenched in Light" was published in *Opportunity*. In this story, the main character, Isis Watts, was based on Hurston's own

OPPORTUNITY
A JOURNAL OF NEGRO LIFE

JUNE
1926

This copy of *Opportunity* magazine, published in June 1926, has an

childhood. And in the dialogue, Hurston reproduced the black dialect that she heard as a child. This dialect writing was similar to that of Paul Lawrence Dunbar.

Like the Civic Club banquet a year earlier, the *Opportunity* dinner was attended by white authors and publishers. Fannie Hurst was very impressed with Hurston. The dinner also featured poets Countee Cullen and Langston Hughes. Hughes received a forty-dollar award for his poem "The Weary Blues." Although he found the money welcome, it was hardly enough for Hughes to support himself. He had to work as a waiter at a hotel in Washington, D.C.

Nevertheless, Hughes's success as a writer took a giant step forward in 1926, when a book of his poetry was published. By that time, he had moved to a rooming house at 267 West 136th Street in Harlem. Hurston also lived in the rooming house, along with other African-American writers. Among the other writers at the house was a twenty-five-year-old named Wallace Thurman. Born in 1901 in Salt Lake City, Utah, Thurman later attended the University of Utah. Before graduating, however, he moved to Los Angeles. There, he started a literary magazine. After the magazine failed, Thurman decided to move to Harlem. He met Langston Hughes, who became his roommate.

Hughes and Thurman represented an important strain of the Harlem Renaissance. In much of their work, they tried to portray African Americans in all their facets. The Talented Tenth had focused on the nobility and intelligence of blacks. Hughes, Thurman, and others also described black nightlife, jazz clubs, criminals, and skin color. Thurman compared his dark color to those African Americans considered to be part of the Talented Tenth. He thought most of the Talented Tenth were light-skinned.

In his novel *The Blacker the Berry*, he wrote about how Lou began to feel that her luscious black complexion was somewhat of a liability, and that her marked color variation from the other people in her environment was a decided curse. Not that she minded being black, being a Negro necessitated having a colored skin, but she did mind being too black."[5]

In 1926, Thurman and Hughes published a new magazine. It was dedicated to the themes that they believed were most important in African-American literature. Called *Fire!!*, the magazine included writing by Thurman, Hughes, Cullen, and Hurston. They designed it to shock the more conservative African Americans. Black leaders like W. E. B. Du Bois did not like *Fire!!* They felt that the articles presented the negative side of the African-American experience.

The new magazine failed to attract a wide audience. Each copy also cost one dollar, considered very expensive at the time. Thurman and Hughes were forced to stop

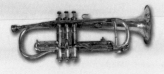
publishing the magazine after only one issue. After its closing, Thurman then started another magazine, called *Harlem*. It was also meant to be a voice for younger writers. However, it closed after only two issues. Nevertheless, *Fire!!* and *Harlem* signaled a new direction for the Harlem Renaissance.

Shades of Black and White

By the mid 1920s, Harlem was in style not only among African Americans but for whites as well. Publications like *The New Negro* helped begin a march uptown from mid-Manhattan to Harlem. Thousands of white Americans came to Harlem to experience its nightlife.

One of the white trendsetters who helped popularize Harlem and the Harlem Renaissance was Carl Van Vechten. Van Vechten—known as Carlo—had grown up in Mississippi. Later he moved to New York City, where he became the music critic for *The New York Times*. He took a deep interest in jazz, which many African-American performers played. At his Manhattan apartment, Van Vechten hosted dinners that included black and white cultural leaders. Leading white publishers, like Alfred A. Knopf, mingled with black writers, like Jessie Fauset and W. E. B. Du Bois. Van Vechten had also become a strong supporter of the Harlem Renaissance and attended the *Opportunity* awards dinner.

Not only did Van Vechten appreciate fine literature, but he was also a best-selling novelist himself. He published a book called *Nigger Heaven* in 1926. The title referred to the balcony of movie theaters. There, blacks were forced to sit, separated from whites. The title and the book were and still are very controversial. The novel featured Anatole Longfellow, who spent most of his time chasing women, and Ralph Pettyjohn, a successful crook. They represented the darker side of Harlem. In contrast, there was a female character named Mary Love who symbolized the culture of the Talented Tenth. Finally, Van Vechten wrote about Byron Kasson. He was a writer who had moved to Harlem and fallen for a black woman.[6]

Van Vechten's novel presented an experience different from what most white Americans were familiar with. But the story fascinated many readers. The novel became a huge best-seller, with one hundred thousand copies of the book being sold.[7]

However, the publication of this controversial book created an uproar in the African-American community. Conservatives like W. E. B. Du Bois hated the book and believed it to be completely inaccurate. Du Bois wanted to promote black accomplishments and advertise black achievements. As he said:

> Is not the continual portrayal of the sordid, foolish
> and criminal among Negroes convincing the world

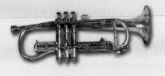

that this and this alone is really and essentially Negroid, and preventing white artists from knowing any other types and preventing black artists from daring to paint them?[8]

But younger writers, like Hughes and Thurman, applauded Van Vechten's book. They believed it was an accurate portrayal of certain parts of Harlem life. They encouraged African-American writers to portray all aspects of black culture. However, Hughes also saw the problems for black writers in presenting the exotic. As he wrote, "In the first place, Negro books are considered by editors and publishers as exotic. Magazine editors will tell you, 'We can use but so many Negro stories a year' (That 'so many' meaning very few.) Publishers will say, 'We already have one Negro novel on our list this fall.'"[9]

Nevertheless, Van Vechten's novel did increase the interest among white Americans in black poetry and novels.[10]

The lifestyle that Van Vechten portrayed appealed to many white New Yorkers. Harlem represented a place where they could enjoy a fast-paced nightlife, some of it illegal. In 1920, the United States had adopted Prohibition, which banned liquor. Nevertheless, many Americans continued to drink. Alcohol was served illegally at clubs called speakeasies. Many of these speakeasies opened in Harlem during the 1920s. They

sance Dancers

376, Bill "Bojangles" Robinson supported himself as a y
g in nightclubs in Washington, D.C. He soon became
tap dancer. After returning from World War I, Robins
revues. He became widely known for one of his acts,
down a staircase. The New York newspapers said that
oking Robinson was the greatest of all tap dancers.
other popular dancer of the period was Earl "Snakehip
ade a name for himself because of his unusual style o
s hips back and forth. Tucker performed regularly at
was called the "human boa constrictor."

1944, tap dancer Bill "Bojangles" Robinson leads youn
ncers in the "Charleston Walk" in New York City. Robin
t his start during the Harlem Renaissance.

attracted partygoers from across New York. Harlem became a destination for people who were looking for a good time. Zora Hurston called Van Vechten one of the "Negrotarians"—her term for whites that supported the Harlem Renaissance.

Many whites headed to Harlem because it had become the center of the most famous nightclubs in New York. Some of them were open only to whites. The most glittering was the Cotton Club on 142nd Street. It featured a lavish floor show with African-American dancers and the band of Edward Kennedy "Duke" Ellington. Known as "Duke" because of his elegant clothes, the tall, handsome Ellington was one of the most popular jazz musicians of the 1920s.

The Twenties has sometimes been called the Jazz Age. Jazz originated in the United States among African-American musicians around the beginning of the twentieth century. Jazz is a type of music that has improvisation and swing. Improvisation means that the musician or singer composes a melody at the same time that he or she is performing it. Swing is the rhythm used in jazz. This rhythm makes the music seem to float as audiences listen to it. Duke Ellington became famous not only as a bandleader but also as a great songwriter. He wrote such jazz standards as "Mood Indigo" and "Sophisticated Lady." He also performed "Take the

Duke Ellington (right) and Louis Armstrong have a few laughs. Ellington led the band at the Cotton Club during the Harlem Renaissance. Although Armstrong spent most of the 1920s in Chicago, he did spend about a year in Harlem playing in Fletcher Henderson's band.

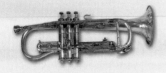

The Lindy dance's popularity endured long after the Harlem Renaissance ended. Above, a couple takes part in a Lindy contest at the Savoy Ballroom in New York in 1953.

A-Train." This was the name of the subway line that people took to the Harlem nightclubs.

In addition to Ellington, the Cotton Club featured other great African-American musicians. These included trumpeter Louis Armstrong as well as singers Ethel Waters and Cab Calloway. Aside from the Cotton Club, white visitors to Harlem went to Connie's Inn, The Spider Web, The Bamboo Inn, and The Lenox. But many

Renaissance Singers

Musical revues featured singers as well as dancers. One of the best known was Bessie Smith. Born in Chattanooga, Tennessee in 1894, Bessie lost her parents when she was only a child. To help support her family, which included six children, she and her brother Andrew began performing. He played the guitar, while young Bessie sang. In 1912, she joined the Moses Stokes Theater Company as a dancer. Gradually she also developed a reputation as a blues singer. During the 1920s, she recorded hits like "Down Hearted Blues," becoming a highly paid entertainer. Smith sang with the Louis Armstrong and Fletcher Henderson bands. In 1937, Smith lost her arm as a result of a severe car accident and died the same year.

Another well-known singer during the Harlem Renaissance was Ethel Waters. Born in Chester, Pennsylvania, in 1896, she grew up in a poor family. Ethel obtained her first job at a hotel. But after performing in a Philadelphia talent contest, she decided to head for New York. During the Harlem Renaissance, Waters became a popular recording artist and appeared with the Duke Ellington Orchestra. She recorded such hits as "Down Home Blues," and "Oh, Daddy." The record label was Black Swan, managed by Fletcher Henderson.

Waters later went on tour with Henderson's band. She was also cast in Broadway musical revues, including one called *Blackbirds of 1930*. During the 1930s and 1940s, she continued recording. Waters starred in Broadway shows and appeared in some films. For one of her performances, she received an Academy Award nomination for Best Supp-

Bessie Smith was a very popular singer in the 1920s and 1930s. This

people preferred the integrated nightclubs—where black and white couples danced. Among the most famous was the Savoy Ballroom on Lenox Avenue between 140th and 141st streets. Its dazzling chandelier lighted the way to a huge dance floor—250 feet by 50 feet. When the Savoy opened on March 12, 1927, four thousand people came for opening night. They danced the Charleston—a popular 1920s dance that went with a song written by James Johnson. The music was provided by clarinetist Stanley "Fess" Williams and his band.

Also featured at the Savoy was the Fletcher Henderson band. Henderson was born in Louisiana, where he learned to play the piano from his mother. He was known as the "King of Swing." His band boasted some of the finest jazz musicians of the era. At one time or another, Louis Armstrong played in the band as well as the pianist Thomas "Fats" Waller. The Fletcher Henderson band also featured such jazz singers as Alberta Hunter.

In addition to nightclubs, people came to Harlem to attend shows. These were known as musical reviews, featuring singers and dancers. Revues had begun on Broadway, then moved uptown to Harlem. Some of the music was composed by James Reese Europe. He had led the band of the 369th Infantry down Broadway after World War I. Another successful songwriter of the period was Noble Sissle, a drummer in the band. Sissle teamed

Rent Parties

Harlem was fashionable in the 1920s, and apartment rents were high. A monthly apartment rent might be as much as fifty-five dollars. This amounted to about one half of a family's income. Rents in Harlem were over twenty dollars more than whites were paying in other parts of New York.[11] Many people living in Harlem did not make the salaries of top stage performers. Therefore, it was difficult for them to afford to pay rents. As a result, they began to hold rent parties.

Harlemites had invitations printed by traveling printers. They pulled up to a building and printed cards. They might say "Railroad Men's Ball at Candy's Place, Friday, Saturday & Sunday, April 29–30, May 1, 1927."[12] When partygoers arrived, usually after midnight, they were asked to pay twenty-five cents for an evening's fun. This might include food, illegal alcohol, a piano player, and a rented piano, paid for by the host or hostess. If they could not afford a live musician, then they might get by with the radio that played music from one of the clubs. Radio helped spread the popularity of jazz bands to people around the country.

Fifty to one hundred people might attend the party. The money they paid went a long way toward the month's rent. However, many people in Harlem lived in such run-down apartments that they could not host a rent party. A report issued in the twenties concluded that Harlem was becoming a "slum." Most of the property was owned by white landlords, who accounted for 80 percent of the community's wealth.[13]

James VanDerZee took this picture of three women out for a walk in Harlem. They are wearing the typical fashions of the 1920s.

up with songwriter Eubie Blake to produce many popular songs. Another veteran of the 369th was Bill "Bojangles" Robinson. He was considered one of the greatest tap dancers of the 1920s.

Harlemania

The wild popularity of Harlem created a phenomenon known as Harlemania. One of the leaders of Harlemania was A'Lelia Walker. A millionairess, Walker was six feet tall and known for her exotic clothes. She was the daughter of Madame C. J. Walker who had made a fortune in hair care and beauty products for African-American women. A'Lelia Walker maintained a mansion outside of New York City on the Hudson River. She also owned a magnificent apartment in Harlem. It was decorated with expensive furniture from Europe, fine paintings, and plush carpets. Walker called her sumptuous salon "The Dark Tower." This was the title of a poem by Countee Cullen. Walker had a framed copy of it on one of her walls.

Cullen, Hughes, and other writers were regular guests at her apartment. She provided them with free meals as well as generous financial support. White society leaders like Carl Van Vechten also attended her parties. Black musicians played for the guests, who included many richly dressed African Americans. As one person who attended her parties later wrote, "You have never

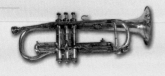

seen such clothes. . . . They do not stop at fur coats made of merely one kind of fur. They add collars of ermine to gray fur, or black fur collars to ermine. Ropes of jewels and trailing silks of all bright colors."[14]

The Harlem Renaissance gave African Americans like A'Lelia Walker an opportunity to be proud of their success. Harlem had become the rage. Going uptown to Harlem was a popular fad that attracted many New Yorkers and out-of-towners. The popularity of Harlem helped bring success to the writers, entertainers, and artists of the Harlem Renaissance.

Chapter 5

Theater and Art

In 1921, **Eubie Blake** and Noble Sissle had a smash hit on Broadway. Called *Shuffle Along*, the musical attracted thousands of New York theatergoers. The song and dance numbers by Blake and Sissle were performed onstage by a highly talented group of actors. They drew wild applause from sold-out audiences. *Shuffle Along* was much like other musicals about African Americans. It featured African Americans singing songs about their lives in the South and "shuffling" along the stage. In this way, the play strengthened the stereotypes that whites had long held about blacks.

But in one way, at least, *Shuffle Along* was different. In the past, musicals had featured white actors. They blackened their faces with burnt cork and pretended to be African Americans. But *Shuffle Along* featured a cast of black actors. This indicated the new roles that blacks were now playing in the American theater. It was part of the success that African Americans achieved during the

Harlem Renaissance. *Shuffle Along* was only one of many black musicals that ran on Broadway during the Harlem Renaissance. African-American actors were usually not happy about the fact that these musicals continued to present the old stereotypes. But they were pleased about having jobs in the theater.

The Growth of African-American Theater

Several actors from *Shuffle Along* went on to have notable careers. One of them was Josephine Baker. Born in St. Louis in 1906, Baker's original name was Freda Josephine McDonald. Her ancestors were black slaves and American Indians. Freda began dancing as a child and appeared in chorus lines as a teenager. She left St. Louis as the Harlem Renaissance began, drawn to the Broadway stage. Calling herself Josephine Baker, she auditioned for *Shuffle Along*. She received a part and appeared in the chorus line. Noble and Sissle also cast her in their 1924 musical *The Chocolate Dandies*.

Baker possessed a unique comic talent as a dancer. With her long limbs and limber form, she often danced at the end of the chorus line. Baker pretended to have forgotten her steps. This drew laughs and applause from audiences. At the end of the dance number, she suddenly seemed to remember what she was supposed to do. Then she got in step with the rest of the line.

During the mid 1920s, Baker left New York and traveled to Paris where she performed at the Theatre des Champs-Elysees. Baker became an instant hit with Parisian audiences. In her exotic acts, she often appeared onstage with a pet leopard called Chiquita. Baker also toured other European capitals. She popularized the music and dance numbers of the Harlem Renaissance.

Two other actresses who appeared in *Shuffle Along* were Adelaide Hall and Florence Mills. Hall became famous as a singer at Harlem's Cotton Club, where she performed with the Duke Ellington Band. Later, she sung on stage with the touring Blackbirds in England. This group also featured the dancer Bill "Bojangles" Robinson.

Florence Mills was born in 1896 in Washington, D.C. Her parents were former slaves. As a child, she began appearing in vaudeville acts. Vaudeville was a type of variety show that included songs, dance numbers, skits, and comedy acts. By 1910, Florence and her family had moved to New York. There she began appearing in vaudeville as part of the "The Mills Sisters," an act that also included her two older sisters. She also appeared with a jazz band called the Tennessee Ten. The band was led by Ulysses "Slow Kid" Thompson. In 1920, Mills and Thompson performed in a musical show called *Folly Town*. It featured white and black actors. But it was as

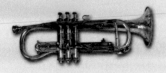
one of the stars in *Shuffle Along* in 1921 that Mills became famous.

From Broadway, Mills became the featured performer of her own show at Harlem's Plantation Restaurant. British promoter C. B. Cochran saw her at the Plantation Restaurant and persuaded Mills to come to England in 1923. At first, she was not accepted by the British as the equal of a white performer. But Mills overcame this prejudice and became a big hit. Like Baker and Hall, she helped popularize the music of the Harlem Renaissance in Europe.

Later Mills toured England as part of the Blackbirds. However, her nonstop pace eventually exhausted her. Returning to Harlem in 1927, she became ill and died suddenly. As author Bill Egan wrote, "The passionate conviction that drove Florence Mills was her belief she could use her talent for entertainment to help break down the barriers of prejudice that was holding back her people. There was no personal bitterness in her hatred of prejudice, just a conviction that it was wrong and illogical."[1]

Another performer who tried to break down these prejudices was Paul Robeson. Born in Princeton, New Jersey, in 1898, Robeson was the son of a Presbyterian minister and a schoolteacher. His outstanding performance in high school won him a scholarship to Rutgers University. There he distinguished himself as the first

One of Paul Robeson's biggest roles was playing the title character in a Broadway production of *Othello* by William Shakespeare.

African-American player on the varsity football team. As a result of his high grades, he was admitted to the academic honor society, Phi Beta Kappa. In 1919, Robeson graduated first in his class at Rutgers. After receiving a law degree from Columbia University in New York City, Robeson joined a prestigious firm. However, according to the Paul Robeson Cultural Center, he "left the firm and the practice of law when a white secretary refused to take dictation from him."[2]

Robeson had always been a gifted speaker. He began acting after leaving the legal profession. During the 1920s, serious plays about African Americans were beginning to appear on the New York stage. They were primarily written by white playwrights, such as Eugene O'Neill. With his rich, deep voice and handsome figure, Robeson seemed perfect for the leading roles. In 1924, he played the lead in O'Neill's *All God's Chillun Got Wings*.

A year later Robeson starred in O'Neill's *The Emperor Jones*. This play tells the story of an African-American man who escapes prison and makes himself emperor of a Caribbean island. In 1928, Robeson appeared in the musical *Showboat*. This is a story that takes place in the South and has black and white characters that fall in love. Robeson was widely identified with his performance of "Ol' Man River" in the musical. This is a song about the Mississippi River.

Like W. E. B. Du Bois, Robeson became a leader in the fight against racism. The roles that he played in *Showboat* and *The Emperor Jones* emphasized the importance of presenting African Americans as real people, not as stereotypes. As Robeson wrote later, "We are too self-conscious, too afraid of showing all phases of our life—especially those phases which are of greatest dramatic value."[3]

So far these "phases of our life" had only been portrayed by white writers. However, during the Harlem Renaissance, they were also depicted by African-American writers. As W. E. B. Du Bois stated in an issue of *The Crisis*, "Negro theater must be: I. About Us. That is, they must have plots which reveal Negro life as it is. II. By us. That is, they must be written by Negro authors who understand from birth and continual association just what it means to be a Negro today."[4]

In 1927, African Americans developed the Harlem Experimental Theater. Jessie Fauset and other participants in the Harlem Renaissance founded the theater. The theater actors performed new plays written by African Americans at the 135th Street Branch Library in Harlem. However, only one play written by African Americans made it to Broadway during the Harlem Renaissance. This was the play *Harlem*, written by Wallace Thurman and William Rapp. It appeared on Broadway in 1929. In this play, Thurman presented both

the positive and negative sides of African-American life in Harlem.

Renaissance Artists

While some artists were appearing onstage, others were busy working in their studios. In the past, African-American painters had faced many hurdles. Art schools discriminated against African Americans, barring them from entry. Black painters also found that most galleries would not accept their work. However, for the first time, the Harlem Renaissance brought the paintings of black artists to the attention of the white public.

One of the earliest black artists of the twentieth century was Meta Vaux Warrick Fuller. An accomplished sculptor, she was best known for her work *Ethiopia Awakening*, completed in 1914. This work depicts a woman wearing clothing in the style of the ancient Egyptians. In much of her work, Fuller explored the influences of Africa on black culture in America. Another famous work by Fuller is *Mary Turner: A Silent Protest*. It was completed in 1919, just before the Harlem Renaissance began. In this highly expressive work, Fuller recalled the tragic life of a pregnant black woman. The sculptor portrayed Mary Turner courageously maintaining her dignity as she was lynched by a white mob. Her lynching occurred after she accused a Georgia lynch mob of wrongfully taking her husband's life. The enraged mob thought he had murdered a white farmer.

W. E. B. Du Bois and James Weldon Johnson saw in Fuller's work an effort to break away from African-American stereotypes. They encouraged other artists to follow the same path. Perhaps the best-known artist of the Harlem Renaissance was Aaron Douglas. Born in Topeka, Kansas, in 1900, Douglas attended the University of Nebraska. After studying with German illustrator Winold Reiss, Douglas became inspired by African art. His African themes appealed to Du Bois and Alain Locke. They wanted other artists to go back to their African roots in their painting.

Douglas painted pictures that appeared in *The Crisis*, as well as in *Opportunity* and other magazines. He also drew illustrations that appeared in *The New Negro*, which had been released in 1925. Some of his later works portrayed the overland journey taken by thousands of African Americans from the South to the cities of the North. Known as the Father of Black American Art, Douglas later began the art department at Fisk University. Beginning in 1937, he remained at Fisk for almost thirty years.

Another leading artist of the Harlem Renaissance was Richard Bruce Nugent. Born in Washington, D.C., in 1906, Nugent grew up in a middle-class family. His mother was a teacher and pianist. When he was still a young

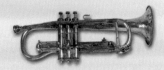

This oil on canvas by Aaron Douglas is called *Aspects of Negro Life: From Slavery to Reconstruction*. It was painted in 1934, toward the end of the Harlem Renaissance.

man, Nugent met the poet Langston Hughes. Hughes recognized Nugent's talent as a writer and artist and encouraged him to publish his work. According to one of his biographies, "Shadows," Nugent's first published poem, was rescued from the trash by Langston Hughes and was eventually sent to the *Opportunity* magazine."[5]

Nugent's first short story appeared in *The New*

Negro.[6] Meanwhile, Nugent was also drawing. During part of the Harlem Renaissance, he lived in the same house of artists and writers as Langston Hughes and Zora Neale Hurston. He drew some of his pictures on the walls of the rooming house. Wearing a gold bead in one ear, he was well known by Harlemites as he roamed the streets of their community. Two of his drawings were published in the only issue of *Fire!!* As Langston Hughes wrote, "Bruce Nugent took it [*Fire!!*] around New York on foot and some of the Greenwich Village bookshops put it on display, and sold it for us. But then Bruce, who had

The Janitor Who Paints by **Palmer Hayden** showed a regular working man who pursued a creative life at home.

no job, would collect the money and, on account of salary, eat it up before he got back to Harlem."[7] In addition, Nugent was the associate editor of another magazine, *Harlem: A Forum of Negro Life*. Only one issue was published in 1928.

Two other artists who produced some of their work during the Harlem Renaissance were Palmer Hayden and Augusta Savage. Palmer Hayden grew up in Virginia, where he worked on the railroad. Eventually he moved to New York, where his subjects became the people of Harlem. One of his paintings, *The Janitor Who Paints*, depicted Cloyde Boykin. He was a painter who had to work as a janitor to survive. "I painted it because no one called Cloyde a painter," Hayden said, "they called him a janitor."[8]

Like Meta Fuller, Augusta Savage was a sculptor. Born in Florida in 1892, she developed an interest in sculpting as a child. However, her father, a Methodist minister, did not support her ambition to become a sculptor. Nevertheless, Savage continued to sculpt. In 1919, she won a prize for one of her works at a county fair. In the early 1920s, Savage moved to New York. There she established herself as an artist and teacher.

A sculpture called *The Harp* depicted one of Savage's favorite themes. It shows an African American in front of a large harp. Savage liked to portray the influence of black music in her sculptures. Savage also

The Harmon Foundation

The Harmon Foundation provided fellowships to African Americans, just like the Rosenwald Foundation. Many recipients were artists. In 1928, the foundation hosted an exhibit of African-American art in New York City. The works of Aaron Douglas, Palmer Hayden, Augusta Savage, and others were featured at the exhibit. The foundation also organized traveling exhibitions of African-American art. As a result, many Americans outside of New York could see the works of black painters, sculptors, and photographers. People who attended the shows could also purchase any of the works that appealed to them. These sales helped provide financial support for black artists.

became known for her sculptured portraits of African Americans. One of her works, called *Gamin*, was a sculpture of her nephew. In 1929, she won the prestigious Julius Rosenwald Fellowship for *Gamin*. Rosenwald was a wealthy philanthropist who was a part-owner of Sears, Roebuck & Company. His foundation provided fellowships (financial aid) to African-American artists and college students. As a result of her fellowship, Savage could afford to study for a year in Paris. After her return, she continued to produce sculpture and teach during the 1930s in Harlem.

Harlem was also home to the most famous photographer of the Harlem Renaissance—James VanDerZee. Prior to becoming a professional photographer, he had a varied career. Growing up in Virginia, he took

Children at a Harlem elementary school pose for a picture by James VanDerZee.

lessons on the violin and piano. In fact VanDerZee became such an accomplished musician that he later played with the Fletcher Henderson jazz band. He also became a violin and piano teacher. In 1915, VanDerZee found a job with a photographer in Newark, New Jersey. He worked in the darkroom, where photographs were developed using chemicals. Sometimes he filled in for the photographer, taking portraits and enlarging them.

A year later, VanDerZee moved to Harlem where he opened a studio, Guarantee Photos. Over the next decade, he took many pictures of day-to-day life in Harlem. Some of them were family portraits of Harlem residents. Others were funerals of people who lived in the community. Among his subjects were famous residents of Harlem such as Adam Clayton Powell, Sr., and A'Lelia Walker. Through his photographs, VanDerZee helped provide a chronicle of the Harlem Renaissance.

Augusta Savage's *Gamin* is a bust of an African-American boy. Savage sculpted the boy's shape with plaster, then painted over it.

Chapter | 6 |

End of an Era

I n 1929, Zora Neale Hurston returned to New York
from a trip to the South, where she had been born.
Hurston had been collecting folklore—traditional
stories that are not always completely true—about African
Americans. Based on these stories, she planned to write a
new book.

Not only was Hurston a gifted novelist, but she also
had become a trained anthropologist. During the 1920s,
she had won a scholarship to Barnard College in New York
City. There, she studied under a leading anthropologist
named Franz Boas.

In 1927, around the same time that she graduated from
Barnard, Hurston met a wealthy woman named Charlotte
van der Veer Quick Mason. The silver-haired Mason had
long been fascinated by the folklore of American Indians
and African Americans. After attending a lecture by Alain
Locke, Mason began to provide financial support to
African-American writers and artists. Among them were
Langston Hughes and Aaron Douglas. Locke became

Mason's adviser, helping her find talented African Americans. He introduced her to Zora Neale Hurston. Mason agreed to provide Hurston with two hundred dollars each month and a car for her trip south. In return, Hurston agreed not to publish any of the folklore unless Mason gave her approval.[1]

Mason was a member of the group that Hurston called the Negrotarians. These were wealthy white patrons who provided financial support to the members of the Harlem Renaissance. Most of these writers and artists could not earn enough from their work to support themselves. For example, Mason provided Langston Hughes with $150 per month, beginning late in 1927, and bought him fancy clothes.[2] As Hughes later recalled, "My patron . . . was a beautiful woman, with snow-white hair and a face that was wise and very kind. . . . She had great sums of money, and had used much of it in great and generous ways. . . . I was fascinated by her, and I loved her."[3]

Others who came in contact with Mason found her controlling. She insisted she be called "godmother." Mason required Hughes and others to sit on the floor at her feet, while she lounged in a large chair.

The 1920s was a period of tremendous financial prosperity for Mason and many other people. American entrepreneurs made money opening new businesses. Many other Americans grew rich investing in the New

From left to right, writers Jessie Fauset, Langston Hughes, and Zora Neale Hurston stand near a statue of African-American activist Booker T. Washington.

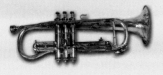

York stock market. Indeed, stock trading became very popular, with small investors hoping to get rich in the market. And some did. As a result, more and more people could afford to go out in the evenings to nightclubs, attend plays, or purchase books and works of art. This new prosperity had helped fuel the Harlem Renaissance.

On Thursday, October 24, 1929—not too long after Zora Hurston returned from her travels—the prosperity bubble burst. The New York Stock Exchange crashed. Five billion dollars was lost in the market within three days. Three weeks later, $30 billion had disappeared from the stock exchange. The impact rolled across the American economy like a tidal wave. Banks, which had invested their deposits in the market, closed their doors. Depositors lost their life savings. Businesses went bankrupt, laying off hundreds of thousands of people. By January 1930, unemployment had reached 4 million workers.

Impact on Harlem

At first, the economic decline did not seem to affect the Harlem Renaissance. In 1930, for example, Langston Hughes published a new book of poetry, *Not Without Laughter*. That same year, James Weldon Johnson released his new book, *Black Manhattan*. In the book, Johnson wrote about the development of Harlem as the center of an African-American cultural renaissance.

A'Lelia Walker

Average workers were not the only ones affected by the Depression. Well-to-do African Americans also felt its impact. Among them was A'Lelia Walker, who had been left a fortune by her mother, along with the family business, a large hair-care products company. As black families lost their incomes, they could no longer afford hair-care and beauty products. Walker sold one of her magnificent homes to support herself. But she did not stop hosting parties, enjoying expensive meals, or buying clothes. After one meal early in the morning of August 17, 1931, Walker suffered a fatal heart attack.

Her funeral was one of the largest ever seen in Harlem. The Reverend Adam Clayton Powell, Sr., led the ceremony. It included a poem composed by Langston Hughes to pay tribute to Walker. So all who love laughter," he wrote:

And joy and light.
Let your prayers be as roses
For this queen of the night."

As Hughes recalled afterward, "That was really the end of the gay times of the New Negro era in Harlem."[4]

As Johnson put it, "Perhaps it was now time for New York again to sing and dance and laugh with the Negro on the stage; and it soon had the opportunity."[5]

Meanwhile, Republican President Herbert Hoover confidently announced that the economy was solid. Americans, Hoover assured, had no need to worry. But the market crash actually signaled the beginning of a long economic depression. Unemployment continued

to increase, and Harlem was hit hardest. African Americans, who held low-paying jobs such as janitors and waiters, were among the first to be laid off. Unemployment in Harlem soared to five times the average in the rest of New York City.[6]

The economic hardships of America cast a shadow over the entire Harlem Renaissance. Financial support for Harlem Renaissance artists began to disappear. Langston Hughes, for instance, had never made much money from his writings. He depended on part-time jobs and received scholarships. These dried up.

In 1930, his relationship with Charlotte Mason also ended. As Hughes looked around and saw the economic plight of black workers, he became frustrated with American society. In his poem "Advertisement for the Waldorf-Astoria," Hughes wrote about whites dancing at a plush hotel while blacks went hungry. Mason did not share Hughes's views. As she said of the poem, "It's not you. It's a powerful poem! But it's not you."[7] She had encouraged Hughes and Hurston to work together on a new folk comedy called *Mule Bone*. Mason provided them with financial support while they wrote. But Hughes and Hurston were unable to work together. Hughes tried to explain the situation to Mason, but she would not listen to him. She stopped giving him money.

In the meantime, Hurston insisted that *Mule Bone* was her work and that Hughes had no claim to it. "It was my story from beginning to end," she said. "It was my dialogue, my situations." By 1931, the long friendship between Hughes and Hurston, which had begun during the 1920s, came to an end. A year later, Hurston ended her relationship with Charlotte Mason and decided to publish her folktales. In 1935, she released her book based on the stories she had collected in the South. It was titled *Mules and Men*. Two years later, she released her finest novel, *Their Eyes Were Watching God*. It was based on her experiences growing up in Eatonville, Florida.

The relationship between Mason, Hughes, and Hurston was an important aspect of the Harlem Renaissance. Mason provided the money that helped them write. The breakup of the three weakened the movement. The Depression also made a major economic impact on Harlem. As Hughes stated, "we were no longer in vogue, anyway, we Negroes. . . . Colored actors began to go hungry, publishers politely rejected new manuscripts, and patrons found other uses for their money."[8]

As the economy worsened, a majority of voters lost faith in the Republicans. In 1932, Democrat Franklin D. Roosevelt was elected president of the United States. Roosevelt and the Democratic Congress had pledged to give Americans a "New Deal." This New Deal program included government efforts to provide jobs for people

who were out of work. Roosevelt had also promised to repeal Prohibition, which soon ended in 1933.

The end of Prohibition devastated Harlem nightlife. Whites saw no reason to come north to Harlem; they could drink legally in midtown Manhattan. As a result, the Harlem speakeasies and many nightclubs closed. More people who lived in Harlem were thrown out of work. They joined the long lines in front of the local churches, which provided food and clothing to the poor.

What Happened to the Writers and Artists

Langston Hughes did not wait to see Harlem sink further into misery. In 1932, he paid for an inexpensive cabin aboard an ocean liner and left on a trip to Europe. Hughes visited the Soviet Union, which was a communist country. Under communism, the government ran the economy, providing every citizen with a job. After touring Europe, Hughes returned to Harlem, where he continued writing. In 1933, he published a book of short stories called *The Ways of White Folks*. It was one of the last literary works of the Harlem Renaissance. Hughes continued writing poems and novels for the next thirty years until he died in 1967.

Some of Hughes's later work appeared in *The Crisis*. But, as the Depression worsened, the magazine lost many of its readers. Financial conditions were so bad that W. E. B. Du Bois told Countee Cullen "I have not drawn my salary for several months in order to make things go."[9] Du Bois left the magazine in 1933 to become a professor at Atlanta University. He continued writing and published a series of books on African-American history over the next thirty years. Du Bois died in Ghana, West Africa, in 1963.

As Du Bois left *The Crisis*, Countee Cullen's career as a distinguished writer was ending. His novel *One Way to Heaven*, published in 1932, was not very popular. Meanwhile, his royalties from other books had been declining. These royalties were a percent of the sales an author received from each book that was sold. While his royalties were about $707 in the first half of 1932, they had dropped to $53 by 1934.[10] To support himself, Cullen became a French teacher at DeWitt Clinton High School in New York. He continued to teach until his death thirteen years later.

Other leaders of the Harlem Renaissance had also seen their lives change. Jessie Fauset gave up her job at *The Crisis*, married an insurance man, and lived in Brooklyn, New York. James Weldon Johnson left New York and became a faculty member at Fisk University. He taught there along with Charles S. Johnson and Aaron Douglas. Meanwhile, Wallace Thurman remained in Harlem. After the success of his play *Harlem*, he

Jazz singer and bandleader Cab Calloway sings with his orchestra at the Cotton Club in Harlem in 1935. CBS radio broadcast the performance.

continued to write. But Thurman developed tuberculosis, a disease of the lungs, and died in 1934.

As the leaders of the Harlem Renaissance died or drifted away, the movement ended. Claude McKay returned to Harlem from Europe the same year that Thurman died. In 1933, he published *Banana Bottom*, a

A store owner displayed signs reading a "colored store," which at the time meant the store was owned by African-Americans. This saved the shop from destruction during the Harlem riot on March 19, 1935.

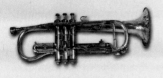
novel about a Jamaican girl named Bita Plant. As he wrote:

> I thank God, although I was brought up and educated among white people, I have never wanted to be anything but myself. I take pride in being colored and different, just as any intelligent white person does in being white. I can't imagine anything more tragic than people torturing themselves to be different from their natural, unchangeable selves.[11]

McKay had hoped to revive the cultural life of the Harlem Renaissance after publishing his novel. But, when he tried to form a "New Negroes Writers Group," no one seemed interested. " . . . we all of us feel more or less at loose ends," he wrote.[12]

As the Depression continued during the 1930s, conditions inside Harlem grew worse. In March 1935, a black boy stole a knife from a store owned by a white merchant in Harlem. Police caught the boy, but word began to spread that he had been brutally beaten. Crowds of African Americans flowed into the streets and began to riot. They targeted white-owned shops in Harlem, which were looted and burned. When the riot finally ended, there had been $2 million worth of damage.[13] By the year of the riot, much of the culture in Harlem had waned.

Chapter 7
Legacy of a Movement

Arna Bontemps, a handsome, broad-shouldered poet and novelist, moved to Harlem during the 1920s. His story illustrates the rise and fall of the Harlem Renaissance. To support himself, he took a teaching position at Harlem Academy. Shortly afterward, his poetry began to appear in *Opportunity* and *The Crisis*. Indeed, his work was so good that both magazines awarded him prizes. After he married Alberta Johnson in 1926, the couple had six children. As he continued to write, Bontemps became part of the Harlem Renaissance circle of poets and novelists. He developed close friendships with Langston Hughes, Countee Cullen, Claude McKay, and others.

But as Harlem began to suffer following the stock market crash in 1929, Bontemps and his family moved south to Huntsville, Alabama. Bontemps had found a new job at Oakwood Junior College, where he taught for three years. In 1932, he published one of his best-known novels,

God Sends Sunday. The main character, Augie, is a black jockey who is experiencing hard times. "Slight in plot," one critic wrote, "the novel is most appreciated for its poetic style, its re-creation of the black idiom [dialect], and the depth of characterization."[1]

Bontemps also began to coauthor children's books with Langston Hughes. But he never gave up writing novels. In 1936, he published a new one titled *Black Thunder*. It is considered his most outstanding work. *Black Thunder* told the story of Gabriel Prosser, who led a slave revolt in Richmond, Virginia, in 1800. Bontemps's final novel, *Drums at Dusk*, was published in 1939. In this book, Bontemps wrote about the successful slave revolt led by Toussaint L'Ouverture in Haiti during the late eighteenth century. However, the book did not sell very well. At this point, Bontemps said, "it was fruitless for a Negro in the United States to address serious writing to my generation."[2] Bontemps turned back to writing children's books. After obtaining a degree in library science in 1943, he took a position as head librarian at Fisk University. He remained there until 1964. From Fisk, he went to Yale University, where he served as head of the Afro-American studies program.

Arna Bontemps was a poet that taught at the Harlem Academy during the 1920s.

Over the next thirty years until his death in 1973, Bontemps became best known as a historian of the Harlem Renaissance. As he put it, he had "a grandstand seat" in Harlem while the movement was in full swing.[3] Bontemps wrote about the leading novelists and poets of the Harlem Renaissance and evaluated their impact.

After the Harlem Renaissance

What was that impact? At first, it did not seem to be long lasting. As the United States became caught up in the Great Depression, the Harlem Renaissance disappeared. For millions of Americans, African-American art and literature seemed less important than finding a job. The focus of the Urban League and the NAACP had changed. Promoting black culture through *Opportunity* and *The Crisis* magazines was far less critical than helping unemployed African Americans feed their families. Harlem itself had been identified with the carefree days of the 1920s. Looking for fun and excitement, many people had traveled to the Harlem nightclubs to drink and dance. Then the bubble burst in 1929. The so-called Roaring Twenties came to an end. The Harlem Renaissance was identified with the past, not with the Depression era of the 1930s.

The Depression also revealed the serious economic

problems confronting Harlem. According to Professor Jeffrey Stewart:

> . . . much of the real estate in Harlem was owned by [white] Americans; and when the depression hit, African Americans lost their jobs at faster rates than [white] Americans, causing foreclosures on mortgages, evictions from rental properties, and a depression and alienation from the American Dream that was expressed violently in the first modern race riot, the Harlem Riot of 1935.[4]

During the late 1930s, many people in Harlem, along with other Americans, began to face poverty.

The Harlem Renaissance was a literary and artistic movement. It never claimed to change American society. What's more, it was a small, local movement. All of that changed with the Great Depression.

After the Harlem Renaissance ended, African Americans had to confront the harsh realities of life in the twentieth-century United States. They still faced discrimination. Their children were forced to attend segregated schools. These schools were generally inferior to those reserved for white children. Blacks were barred from many theaters, restaurants, and hotels, which were designated for whites only. During the 1930s, the federal government began to establish programs to provide jobs for the unemployed. But whites were hired ahead of blacks. Finally, African Americans continued to suffer as victims of violence, especially in the South. White mobs took justice into their own hands and lynched blacks accused of murder and other crimes. These conditions filled Langston Hughes, Arna Bontemps, and other writers with great despair. As Hughes wrote:

What happens to a dream deferred?

Does it dry up
like a raisin in the sun?
Or fester like a sore—
And then run?
Does it stink like rotten meat?

Or crust and sugar over—
like a syrupy sweet?

Maybe it just sags
like a heavy load.

Or does it explode?[5]

The Legacy of the Harlem Renaissance

The black civil rights movement exploded during the 1960s. Led by the Reverend Martin Luther King, Jr., African Americans successfully pushed for new laws that brought them equal rights. Men like W. E. B. Du Bois had laid the foundation for this movement thirty years earlier. During the Harlem Renaissance, writers, performers, and artists asserted a sense of pride in being African Americans. Writers explored the roots of their culture from Africa. They collected folktales from the black experience during slavery. They also explored the African-American identity—what it meant to be black in a culture dominated by whites. The characters of authors and playwrights represented many aspects of Harlem life and were not afraid to use the jargon of average African Americans. Musicians, singers, and dancers popularized jazz, which had sprung from the African-American experience. Artists depicted urban street life

Jonelle Procope (center), president and CEO of the Apollo
Theater Foundation, is joined by Time Warner CEO Dick
Parsons (right) during the unveiling ceremony of the
refurbished Apollo Theater in Harlem on December 15, 2005.

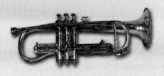

in Harlem and other African-American neighborhoods on their canvases.

The Harlem Renaissance was a major flowering of African-American culture. It was a time when many northern whites had paid close attention to what blacks had to say. While the Harlem Renaissance may have ended in the 1930s, its impact on later African-American artists, writers, and performers continued. For example, some of the performers who flourished during the Harlem Renaissance pursued successful careers long after it ended. Jazz musicians, like Duke Ellington, remained popular for decades. They also influenced other jazz performers, like trumpeter Miles Davis, who rose to fame after them.

Among the most popular clubs of the Harlem Renaissance was the Apollo Theater on West 125th Street. The Apollo remained popular during the following decades. On its stage appeared jazz singers like Billie Holiday and Ella Fitzgerald. They had been influenced by the music of the Harlem Renaissance. They joined other singers whose careers begun during the Harlem Renaissance itself.

Alberta Hunter, for example, had started recording on the Black Swan label with Fletcher Henderson in 1921. During the 1930s, Hunter performed in Paris and traveled to Russia. During World War II, she entertained American troops fighting in Europe. After a brief

Ella Fitzgerald made her professional singing debut at the Apollo Theater in 1934, toward the end of the Harlem Renaissance. She became very popular in the late 1930s and 1940s. Here, she performs at the Savoy Ballroom in 1940.

retirement in the 1950s, she returned to music and continued appearing onstage until her death in 1984.

Ethel Waters also enjoyed a long career. Waters starred on Broadway in *Mamba's Daughters* in 1939. During the 1940s, she appeared in the film *Cabin in the Sky* with Louis Armstrong. Waters's career in the theater continued over the next decade, and she appeared on television during the 1950s.

111

One of the greatest legacies of the Harlem Renaissance was its impact on African-American writers. Alice Walker received a Pulitzer prize for her novel *The Color Purple*, published in 1982. Walker's works describe many areas of the African-American experience. In an interview, she acknowledged her debt to the Harlem Renaissance. Referring to Zora Neale Hurston's novel *Their Eyes Were Watching God*, Walker said, "No book is more important to me than this one." As critic Jace Clayton wrote, "Hurston's tale of self-realization and autonomy is composed with high poetry and thick dialect. [It] is a celebration of black female selfhood and . . . African-American culture." This same theme is explored in *The Color Purple*.[6]

Another writer who was influenced by the Harlem Renaissance is Toni Morrison. The Pulitzer prize-winning Morrison, "more than any other contemporary author . . . carries Jean Toomer's literary torch," according to Clayton. Like Toomer's novel *Cane*, Morrison's story *Jazz* focuses on the lives of African-American women. Her novel takes place in Harlem during the twenties, the period of the Harlem Renaissance.

The success of black writers in the Harlem Renaissance inspired other novelists, like Ralph Ellison. Ellison came to Harlem in the 1930s. There, he met Langston Hughes, Alain Locke, and novelist Richard Wright. These relationships inspired him to become a professional writer. Ellison went to work for the Federal Writer's Project. This was a government program established to employ writers during the Great Depression. He worked for the Living Lore Unit, collecting folk stories from the African-American experience. Perhaps his best-known work is *The Invisible Man*, published in 1952. In this book, Ellison described the experiences of an African American's search for his identity and

Painter Jacob Lawrence captured the spirit of Harlem Renaissance nightlife in his work entitled *Many Whites Come to Harlem to Watch the Negroes Dance.*

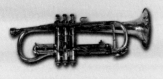
self-awareness. This book explored many of the same themes that emerged during the Harlem Renaissance.

The Harlem Renaissance was a major era in the history of the United States. For approximately fifteen years, a unique group of artists, writers, and performers flourished in Harlem. Harlem briefly became one of the leading cultural centers of America. The leaders of this renaissance produced an outstanding body of work that has enriched American culture. They influenced later African-American writers and artists and made a lasting impact on the cultural traditions of the United States.

TIMELINE

1910 — W. E. B. Du Bois becomes editor of *The Crisis* magazine.

1912 — James Weldon Johnson publishes *The Autobiography of an Ex-Colored Man*.

1919 — 369th Infantry marches up Fifth Avenue to Harlem; Jessie Redmon Fauset becomes editor at *The Crisis*.

1921 — *Shuffle Along*, a black musical revue, is performed.

1922 — Claude McKay publishes *Harlem Shadows*.

1923 — *Opportunity* magazine is founded by the Urban League; Jean Toomer publishes *Cane*; The Cotton Club opens in Harlem.

1924 — Civic Club dinner launches New Negro movement; Jessie Fauset publishes *There is Confusion*; Walter White publishes *The Fire in the Flint*.

1925 — *Opportunity* holds first awards dinner; *The Crisis* holds first awards ceremony.

1926 — Savoy Ballroom is opened; Wallace Thurman publishes *Fire!!*; Langston Hughes publishes

The Weary Blues; Carl Van Vechten publishes *Nigger Heaven*.

1927— A'Lelia Walker opens "The Dark Tower."

1928— Claude McKay publishes *Home to Harlem*.

1929— Wallace Thurman's play *Harlem* opens; stock market crashes; Depression begins.

1930— James Weldon Johnson publishes *Black Manhattan*.

1931— A'Lelia Walker dies.

1932— Langston Hughes and others travel to the Soviet Union.

1933— Claude McKay publishes *Banana Bottom*; Prohibition is repealed.

1934— W. E. B. Du Bois leaves *The Crisis*; Langston Hughes publishes *The Ways of White Folks*.

1935— Race riot erupts in Harlem; Harlem Renaissance ends.

1937— Zora Neale Hurston publishes *Their Eyes Were Watching God*.

Chapter Notes

Chapter 1. Marching in Harlem

1. Richard Slotkin, *Lost Battalions: The Great War and the Crisis of American Nationality* (New York: Henry Holt, 2005), p. 47.
2. Ibid.
3. Ibid., p. 48.
4. Ibid., p. 113.
5. Ibid., p. 121.
6. Ibid., p. 145.
7. Ibid., p. 172.
8. David Levering Lewis, *When Harlem Was in Vogue* (New York: Knopf, 1981), p. 4.

Chapter 2. Beginnings

1. David Levering Lewis, ed., *Harlem Renaissance Reader* (New York: Viking, 1994), pp. 4–5.
2. W. E. B. Du Bois, "The Souls of Black Folk," *Bartleby.com* 2005, <http://www.bartleby.com/114/1.html> (September 10, 2007).
3. Gerald C. Hynes, "A Biographical Sketch of W. E. B. Du Bois," *W.E.B. Du Bois Learning Center* n.d., <http://www.duboislc.org/html/DuBoisBio.html> (September 10, 2007).
4. W. E. B. Du Bois, *The Souls of Black Folk* (Greenwich, Conn.: Fawcett, 1961), pp. 3–4.
5. W. E. B. Du Bois, "The Souls of Black Folk," *Bartleby.com,* 2005, <http://www.bartleby.com/114/1.html> (September 10, 2007).
6. Hynes.

7. Laban Carrick Hill, *Harlem Stomp! A Cultural History of the Harlem Renaissance* (New York: Little Brown, 2003), p. 36.

8. Cary D. Wintz, ed., *The Emergence of the Harlem Renaissance* (New York: Garland Publishing, 1996), p. 15.

9. Ibid., p. 20.

10. Ibid., p. 22.

11. Wintz, p. 48.

12. Ibid., p. 49.

13. Ibid., p. 23.

14. Laban Carrick Hill, p. 21.

15. W. E. B. Du Bois, "The Talented Tenth," *Yale University* n.d., <http://www.yale.edu/glc/archive/1148.htm> (September 10, 2007).

16. Steven Watson, *The Harlem Renaissance: Hub of African-American Culture, 1920–1930* (New York: Pantheon Books, 1995), p. 19.

17. "Alain LeRoy Locke," *The Black Renaissance*, June 20, 2003, <http://www.dclibrary.org/blkren/bios/lockea.html> (September 10, 2007).

Chapter 3. Writing About the Black Experience

1. Claude McKay, "If We Must Die," *Bartleby.com*, 1922, <http://www.bartleby.com/269/74.html> (November 9, 2007).

2. Cary D. Wintz, ed., *The Emergence of the Harlem Renaissance* (New York: Garland Publishing, 1996), p. 69.

3. Steven Watson, *The Harlem Renaissance: Hub of African-American Culture, 1920–1930* (New York: Pantheon Books, 1995), p. 34.

4. Ibid., p. 38.

5. Claude McKay, "A Negro's Friend," *Mr. Africa's Poetry Lounge*, n.d.,<http://www.ctadams.com/claude mckay10.html> (November 9, 2007).

6. Claude McKay, "The White House," *Poets.org*, ©1997–2007,<http://www.poets.org/viewmedia.php/prmmid/15248> (November 9, 2007).

7. Watson, p. 39.

8. David Levering Lewis, *When Harlem Was in Vogue* (New York: Knopf, 1981), p. 231.

9. Scott Williams, "A Jean Toomer Biography," n.d., <http://www.math.buffalo.edu/~sww/toomer/toomerbio.html> (September 10, 2007).

10. Watson, p. 44.

11. Williams.

12. Jean Toomer, *Cane* (W.W. Norton & Company, 1993), p. 12.

13. Williams.

14. Michael Anderson, "Passing Strange," *Times Literary Supplement*, October 6, 2006, p. 23.

15. Ibid.

16. Lewis, *When Harlem Was in Vogue*, p. 75.

17. Lewis, *The Portable Harlem Renaissance Reader*, p. 243.

18. Lewis, *When Harlem Was in Vogue*, p. 79.

19. Lewis, *The Portable Harlem Renaissance Reader*, pp. 257–258.

20. *The Collected Poems of Langston Hughes* (New York: Knopf, 1994).

Chapter 4. A Flowering of Culture

1. Cary D. Wintz, ed., *The Emergence of the Harlem Renaissance* (New York: Garland Publishing, 1996), p. 179.

2. David Levering Lewis, ed., *The Portable Harlem Renaissance Reader* (New York: Viking, 1994), pp. 339, 341.

3. David Levering Lewis, *When Harlem Was in Vogue* (New York: Knopf, 1981), pp. 94–95.

4. Wintz, p. 101.

5. Lewis, *The Portable Harlem Renaissance Reader*, p. 632.

6. Lewis, *When Harlem Was in Vogue*, p. 97.

7. Amritjit Singh, *The Novels of the Harlem Renaissance* (The Pennsylvania State University Press, 1976), p. 22.

8. Ibid., pp. 28–29.

9. Ibid., p. 26.

10. Wintz, p. 101.

11. Lewis, *When Harlem Was in Vogue.*, p. 108

12. Laban Carrick Hill, *Harlem Stomp! A Cultural History of the Harlem Renaissance* (New York: Little Brown, 2003), p. 78.

13. Lewis, *When Harlem Was in Vogue*, p. 109.

14. Steven Watson, *The Harlem Renaissance: Hub of African-American Culture, 1920–1930* (New York: Pantheon Books, 1995), p. 144.

Chapter 5. Theater and Art

1. Bill Egan, "Florence Mills: A Lost Treasure,"

n.d., <http://www.nathanielturner.com/florencemills. htm> (September 10, 2007).

2. "About Paul Robeson," *The Paul Robeson Cultural Center*, 2005, <http://prcc.rutgers.edu/ Robeson/biography.htm> (September 10, 2007).

3. David Levering Lewis, ed., *The Portable Harlem Renaissance Reader* (New York: Viking, 1994), p. 59.

4. Laban Carrick Hill, *Harlem Stomp! A Cultural History of the Harlem Renaissance* (New York: Little Brown, 2003), p. 112.

5. "Richard Bruce Nugent," *The Black Renaissance in Washington, D.C.*, June 20, 2003, <http://www.dclibrary.org/blkren/bios/nugentrb.html> (September 10, 2007).

6. Ibid.

7. "Richard Bruce Nugent," n.d., <http://fire-press.com/fire/bio5.html> (September 10, 2007).

8. "Palmer Hayden, Harlem Renaissance artist!," *The African American Registry*, 2005, <http://www. aaregistry.com/african_american_history/601/Palmer_ Hayden_Renaissance_ar...> (September 10, 2007).

Chapter 6. End of an Era

1. Steven Watson, *The Harlem Renaissance: Hub of African-American Culture, 1920–1930* (New York: Pantheon Books, 1995), p. 149.

2. Ibid., p. 127.

3. Cary D. Wintz, ed., *The Emergence of the Harlem Renaissance* (New York: Garland Publishing, 1996), p. 181.

4. Watson., pp. 164–165.

5. David Levering Lewis, ed., *The Portable Harlem Renaissance Reader* (New York: Viking, 1994), p. 44.

6. Watson, p. 159.

7. David Levering Lewis, *When Harlem Was in Vogue* (New York: Knopf, 1981), p. 258.

8. Wintz, p. 220.

9. Lewis, *When Harlem Was in Vogue*, p. 241.

10. Wintz, p. 221.

11. Lewis, *When Harlem Was In Vogue*, p. 295.

12. Ibid., p. 224.

13. Wintz, p. 225.

Chapter 7. Legacy of a Movement

1. Robert E. Fleming, "Arna Bontempts Life and Career," March 21, 2001, n.d.,<http://www.english.uiuc.edu/maps/poets/a_f/bontemps/life.htm> (September 10, 2007).

2. Ibid.

3. Cary D. Wintz, ed., *The Emergence of the Harlem Renaissance* (New York: Garland Publishing, 1996), p. 219.

4. "Harlem Renaissance," *Online News Hour*, February 20, 1998, <http://www.pbs.org/newshour/forum/february98/harlem5.html> (September 10, 2007).

5. "Langston Hughes," n.d., <http://en.wikipedia.org/wiki/Langston_Hughes> (September 10, 2007).

6. Jace Clayton, "The Harlem Renaissance," *Infoplease*, n.d.,<http://www.infoplease.com/spot/harlem1.html> (September 10, 2007).

GLOSSARY

American Expeditionary Force (AEF)—The name of the U.S. Army in Europe in World War I.

dialect writing—Literature written in the way a specific group of people speak.

jazz—A type of music that stresses improvisation.

Jim Crow laws—Laws that discriminated against African Americans.

lynch—To put to death by mob action without legal sanction.

Prohibition—Beginning in 1920 and ending in 1933, liquor was banned in the United States under the Eighteenth Amendment to the Constitution.

segregation—The separation of blacks and whites.

speakeasies—Clubs where liquor was illegally served.

Talented Tenth—What W. E. B. Du Bois called the most highly educated African Americans; he believed the top 10 percent most educated African Americans should lead the way to equality.

FURTHER READING

Govenar, Alan. *Stompin' at the Savoy: The Story of Norma Miller.* Cambridge, Mass.: Candlewick Press, 2006.

Hardy, Stephen and Sheila Jackson. *Extraordinary People of the Harlem Renaissance.* New York: Children's Press, 2000.

Haugen, Brenda. *Langston Hughes: The Voice of Harlem.* Minneapolis, Minn.: Compass Point Books, 2006.

Hill, Laban Carrick. *Harlem Stomp! A Cultural History of the Harlem Renaissance.* New York: Little Brown, 2003.

Jordan, Denise. *Harlem Renaissance Artists.* Chicago: Heinemann Library, 2003.

Kallen, Stuart A. *Harlem Jazz Era.* San Diego, Calif.: Lucent Books, 2004.

McKissack, Lisa Beringer. *Women of the Harlem Renaissance.* Minneapolis, Minn.: Compass Point Books, 2007.

Rau, Dana Meachen. *The Harlem Renaissance.* Minneapolis, Minn.: Compass Point Books, 2006.

INTERNET ADDRESSES

Collection Guides & Bibliographies— A Guide to Harlem Renaissance Materials

<http://www.loc.gov/rr/program/bib/harlem/harlem.html>

Harlem 1900–1940: Schomburg Exhibit

<http://www.si.umich.edu/CHICO/Harlem/text/
exhibition.html>

"Harlem Renaissance," Online NewsHour Forum

<http://www.pbs.org/newshour/forum/february98/
harlem5.html>

INDEX